Money Wise

Money Wise
Timeless Lessons on Building Wealth

Deepak Shenoy

JUGGERNAUT BOOKS
C-I-128, First Floor, Sangam Vihar, Near Holi Chowk,
New Delhi 110080, India

First published in hardback by Juggernaut Books 2021
Published in paperback by Juggernaut Books 2023

Copyright © Deepak Shenoy 2021

10 9 8 7 6 5 4 3 2 1

P-ISBN: 9789393986627
E-ISBN: 9789391165413

All material in this book is for informational and educational purposes only, and should not be construed to be financial advice. The author and publisher are not responsible for any losses due to investment decisions taken by the reader. Financial markets involve the possibility of losses. Please contact a registered financial adviser before taking any action on your financial portfolios.

All rights reserved. No part of this publication may be reproduced, transmitted, or stored in a retrieval system in any form or by any means without the written permission of the publisher.

Typeset in Adobe Caslon Pro by R. Ajith Kumar, Noida

Printed at Thomson Press India Ltd

To Dad, my greatest inspiration

Contents

1. Start   1
   The Beginning

2. Mutual Funds   29
   Get someone else to do your investing

3. Walking the Talk   79
   A practical approach to investing

4. Stocks   111
   These things called shares

5. Suckered   175
   Sundry scams and sharp practices

Acknowledgements   245

A Note on the Author   247

START
The Beginning

The story of investing

My father passed away nearly 25 years ago, in 1997. In an effort to finally clear out his effects, I was going through a box of really old papers – some dating back to 1977. This included stuff like our correspondence with the bank he worked for after he passed on, how it all panned out, and so on. It took me a few hours, and I went through a spectrum of emotions as I realized how my dad had invested and saved his money.

He had a loan for a house, topped up with another loan because the builder refused to finish the property unless we paid more. A set of life insurance policies against this loan was also there, as a second security; essentially the house and the life insurance policies were collateral for a housing loan.

And there was another loan against shares taken at nearly 19 per cent interest. He would take his savings and invest them in shares, and to discourage himself from selling, he'd put that as collateral against an account, from which he would draw money for urgent expenditure.

After he passed away, nearly all the 'settlement' received – an untaken leave encashment, gratuity and provident fund, along with the insurance policies – went entirely to pay off the housing loan and the loan against the shares.

At first glance it looked crazy because he made very little as a salary, and very little of that was left to save, and he'd put all of those savings into shares of companies whenever he could. I was working, and my mom had the house, so it wasn't too bad. But it made me realize the implications of having worked thirty-five years, and having very little actual cash left at the end.

But that's not the story. The story is that once we paid up the loans, we may have had very little cash, but we had the shares, now freed from the loan collateral. Mom still has these shares today.

In the next twenty years these shares went on to make my mom more than 50x of what my dad had paid. Now, she gets as much dividend per year as the entire portfolio was valued at in 1997. And all this comes from just eight companies.

My dad bought into a lot more than eight companies. This was a time when people owned physical shares, so I have the share certificates of many companies – some thirty to forty companies in all. Some of these businesses don't even exist any more – they just died. Some have gone private. I guess only 20–25 per cent of the companies we owned continue to be in business. Among the survivors too, some were gobbled up or broken up. Brooke Bond became part of Hindustan Unilever, L&T split into L&T and UltraTech, and so on.

Think it through. Out of nearly forty companies, only eight survived. But those eight have given us superlative returns for over twenty years. If you valued the entire portfolio of forty companies in 1997, the return even with that low survival rate translates to 17.7 per cent for one year compounded over twenty-four years – that's a 50x return.

One key factor here: There was no selling, most of the time. That's largely because for the first few years we had no idea how to sell. After that, there was no inclination to do so either. And there was no attempt to 'rejig' the portfolio, even as the value of the shares swung about. The returns went from 50 per cent up in one stock, to about 35 per cent up in another, while the first big winner reduced in value to half its original price, and so on.

The lessons to be learnt

There are so many lessons here.

The first lesson: Let the money compound. What we call a 'mere' 17 per cent return becomes a phenomenal 50x in twenty-four years. Only 17 per cent? What if it was, say, 15 per cent?

Fifteen per cent would multiply your money 28 times in twenty-four years; 12 per cent would 'only' increase it 15 times. The multiplier you get lowers as returns come down, but it also means something deeper. We probably shouldn't expect those 25 per cent returns that every stock market investor seems to think is their birthright.

Compounding is a brilliant thing. What might seem like a very low number like 12 per cent will still, over a period of 25 years, see Rs 1,00,000 grow to Rs 15,00,000.

The second lesson: Money is made largely when you sleep. If you listen to rumours, then the markets will crash every second year, and you should take your money out. Just doing that takes you out of the game, and you have no idea when to get back in. The end result is that you just watch the markets go all the way up regardless.

Take end 2008. Globally investors were scared because a big Wall Street institution, Lehman Brothers, had gone bankrupt. And there was the fear that the collapse of insurance giant AIG would take the markets down again. Then in December 2008 came another massive scandal. A financier, Bernie Madoff, had falsified reports and essentially scammed his clients of billions of dollars.

The following January in India, Satyam's CEO Ramalinga Raju confessed to having falsified his company's earnings. Stocks across the world continued to free-fall all the way till March 2009.

And then suddenly markets started to go up. There wasn't an easy explanation. Yet markets continued to rise. In financial parlance, there's a saying: Markets climb a wall of worry. They did, and indeed, within three months – by June 2009 – they were up 80 per cent from the bottom.

Your emotions won't let you invest because the market is 'high' – and yet, if you had waited for yet another bottom, it would simply not have come. Most of the money in the markets is made by having a position, not by standing outside the airplane wondering if it's a good time to get in.

The third lesson: You don't need that much money to make money. You can start with nothing, or very little, really.

In today's terms, say you put Rs 3000 per week into an investment. Every week. Without fail. In a bank account. In fifteen years, you will have nearly 32 lakh rupees. (We assume banks will give just 4 per cent per year as interest. You saved Rs 23 lakh, the rest is that tiny bit of interest you've been making.)

As your income goes up every year, so must your savings. Let's say we decide to increase the weekly deposit by 5 per cent a year. First year, you're putting Rs 3000 a week. Second year, it's 3150. Third year, it's about 3300, and so on.

In the same fifteen years, you now have Rs 44 lakh. This is now starting to get serious.

What if you get 10 per cent returns? The stock markets have often done that in the past, and more than that too. At that rate, your Rs 3000 a week with 5 per cent increase every year, goes to Rs 71 lakh rupees in fifteen years.

My father's savings earned a return of 17 per cent. Those were great times, we know, but if the markets do 17 per cent, you'll end up with Rs 1.3 crore in fifteen years. That's a game changer.

This is by using savings that might be relatively small. Many of you won't even notice a Rs 3000 per week saving; and it'll start to grow, while you sleep.

So the ways to making money in the markets are . . .

. . . described in the rest of the book. Remember it's not *the way*. It's many different ways, using many different mechanisms. You don't have to find the one holy grail. The eventual point is to do one thing: Prosper.

The most commonly asked question is: What do I invest in that will make money? This is often the wrong question. Because the answer is: Work and get paid.

This is not me making a silly joke. The first crore you make will largely come from your income, from the work you do. Your profession will pay you a salary, or your business will generate the cash, or you'll join a start-up, which is acquired and, voila, you have some money.

#1: Initially? Focus on earning money. Not returns.

This also means in the first few years of your life, focus on just saving as much as you can. Saving is a complex beast. You can do it meaningfully by just creating fixed deposits each month. This may be supremely inefficient for taxes and all that, but let's not focus on that just yet.

Think of Ansh. He's just starting out in his career. He's earning, say, Rs 25,000 a month. He saves Rs 5000.

You can tell him to invest in the stock market. He puts in his Rs 5000 a month for a year. He's now saved Rs 60,000 – and gets 11 per cent on his investment. Guess what, this adds up to Rs 63,120. That's a total earning of Rs 3120 in a year.

If instead he had put the money in a bank at 5 per cent interest, he would have roughly Rs 61,400 instead. The difference? For a risky 11 per cent return, Ansh made an extra Rs 1700 a year, or about Rs 150 extra a month.

What if the stock market fell? Well, he'd have less than Rs 60,000 in his account and he'd be miserable.

For a mere extra Rs 150 a month, why even bother to take the risk? Let the savings of the first year – hey, even the first two years – be parked entirely in fixed deposits. Build that first little nest egg without taking too much risk.

Now I'm a stock market person who loves taking risks. And I'm telling you not to take the risk. Why? Because of two things:
(a) You take risk when the reward is meaningful. Not for Rs 150 extra per month.
(b) You can focus on building your income instead.

Part (b) is really important. Initially, your savings are meagre because early in the game you typically spend 80 per cent of your income anyhow. If the little you save goes into stocks, and stocks do badly, you'll be miserable. You can use systematic investment plans (SIPs) in mutual funds that invest in stocks and we'll discuss that in detail later. But you'd still be miserable if you check out your portfolio often and find you're losing capital.

Instead if you put the money in fixed deposits or, even better, if you invest the money into learning more about your industry or job, buying courses online, or getting another degree perhaps, you'll get more bang for your buck.

Now let's say Ansh signed on to an online course for Rs 10,000 learning to do internet marketing. And now, he's got a job that pays Rs 50,000 a month. His investment of Rs 10,000 has given him an annual increment of Rs 300,000 (Rs 25,000 more rupees per month). Show me a single mutual fund or stock that might be able to do that.

The point is simple: Initially, **focus on increasing your income.** When you get to a figure that's respectable – say 8 to 10 months of expenses – that's when you start moving incremental money into equity, or into other risky asset classes.

(Oh, and don't think of a house as an investment. It's just something you're going to live in, or use, like your car. It's an expenditure. We'll discuss why.)

This sounds very different from what my father did – he put his tiny savings into stocks. But the unsaid part of the story is that he probably started any real form of investing only after he was thirty-five. Before that, nearly everything he saved would just vanish as running expenses. By the time he was saving, a career path was set. And it wasn't a time when you could invest in your own education. If you had a steady job in a government organization (like a public sector bank) you just had to work x years to get promoted, then work another x years, and so on.

#2: When you have enough money, think about 'allocation'

So our hero Ansh has now saved for two years, and is now earning Rs 50,000 a month, and saving Rs 20,000. His savings have added to an impressive Rs 5,00,000 in the bank.

He's still got to think of a few things:
- An emergency fund of six months of expenses 'just in case'
- The rest can go towards **long-term savings**
- Oh and he's got to fund that trip to Croatia next year. He's going to need Rs 1,50,000 to hang out with his friends.
- Other than that, **long-term savings**

If you think about it, he has some money he can reallocate:
- Ansh can leave Rs 1,80,000 in the bank (for six months of expenses)
- Rs 1,50,000 for the Croatia trip in something that will be safe until he uses it
- This adds up to Rs 3,30,000
- What about the rest – Rs 1,70,000?

This is when Ansh can start thinking about 'allocation' to risky assets. Think of putting your money into different buckets.

In one bucket is the safety of a fixed deposit at a bank: Low (or no) risk

In another is the riskiness of the stock market: High risk

There will be others, but let's focus on this. Till now Ansh had:
- No risk bucket: Rs 5,00,000
- Risk bucket: Rs 0

Now, he can change this:
- No risk bucket: Rs 3,30,000, of which:
  - Emergency (Rs 1,80,000) – this is his parachute
  - Croatia trip (Rs 1,50,000)
- Risk bucket: We have Rs 1,70,000 to allocate

He can do this in several ways. Consider his options.

He can move the entire Rs 1,70,000 to the equity markets through a mutual fund.

Don't forget he's still saving Rs 20,000 a month. He could start moving that to the equity markets too, now that the parachute is taken care of. Let's say he decides to buy some **large-cap index funds**. (We'll discuss this later.)

In a year, he would have invested:
- No risk: Rs 3,30,000
- Risk: Rs 4,10,000
  - Started off with Rs 1,70,000
  - Added Rs 20,000 a month for a year

This is now a 55:45 allocation to no risk vs risk.

He takes the Croatia trip. He now has:
- No risk: Rs 1,80,000
- Risk: Rs 4,10,000

His 'allocation' has changed to 30 per cent no risk, 70 per cent risk. Ansh thinks about this and he doesn't like it. He feels markets are risky. Plus, the no-risk cash is also an emergency fund that he may need to dip into anyhow.

So he plans for his next few months like this:
- Invest the first six months' worth of savings into no-risk, to increase his risk buffer

- For the rest of the year, add savings into the risk bucket

In six months, he would have added Rs 1,20,000 (at 20,000 per month) into the no-risk buffer.

So, after six months adding Rs 20,000 x 6 in no-risk funds:
- No risk: Rs 3,00,000
- Risk: Rs 4,10,000

This is back to 42 per cent no-risk, 58 per cent risk. That's not complicated.

There's another way to do this. If he decides to split his savings, adding Rs 10,000 x 6 into risk and the same into no-risk:
- No risk: Rs 2,40,000
- Risk: Rs 4,70,000

He's back to 34 per cent no-risk, 67 per cent risk. That's not complicated either.

How exactly he chooses to do this depends on his inclinations and life circumstances. Does he have elderly infirm parents, or young kids? Is he DINK, with his parents well settled?

The choice of whether a person can take more risk depends on only two things:
- **Can I take risk?** People with liabilities, dependants or those who don't have a safety net must first focus on having enough in the no-risk bucket to allow them to sleep at night.
- **Must I take risk?** Many of us are naturally unconditioned to risk-taking. Does losing money, even temporarily, scare you? If the answer is a sheepish yes, then a higher amount of money in a risk bucket is unhealthy.

The key idea is to just divide your money into different 'asset classes'. Fixed deposits are an asset class. Stocks are an asset class. You can access both through mutual funds, or directly buy into either one.

There are other asset classes too. Gold. International stocks. Real estate. Start-ups. Chit funds. Cryptocurrency. Commodities like industrial metals. Each one has a different amount of risk attached. Now you could have buckets for all of them.

I would personally recommend using just equity and fixed income for the first few years while you build your nest egg. Add the other asset classes later.

#3: Plan for the absolute necessities

You're going to need to plan for retirement. When you stop working you're going to need a nest egg that is enough for you and your folks. How much is enough to retire? Don't we all want to retire early?

We'll discuss those questions separately in 'Your personal financial plan'.

Oh, we'll also cover the basics around planning for your children's education and all that.

#4: With the rest, enjoy your life

Life is short. And oh, the pandemic has really taught us that it can be a lot shorter than we expected, or hoped for. You can't take your money with you when you go. So whatever you have left, over and above necessities, use it for the things you really want to do.

So go on, spend and enjoy yourself. Your spending also helps to grow the economy, but that's too noble a goal to consider. Just spend for your own happiness. Bring a smile to the face of someone you love. Indulge yourself. A holiday, a new car, or a sabbatical, a fancy home theatre system. All of these things are cool.

If you don't force yourself to spend what you've saved beyond the necessary, you'll end up more unhappy than if you've not saved at all. Fear that you'll die after you've worked your ass off, without a tale to tell.

So every once in a while take that expensive cruise, learn to scuba dive, buy that piano, fly in a higher class than you would normally. For too many of us, spending comes easy when it's little amounts: instead of a phone that costs 20,000 we'll buy an iPhone or something like that. But spend 5,00,000 on a trip to Wimbledon? Maybe not. But which splurge will have made you feel more alive?

Why should you invest at all? To build personal leverage

Focusing on earning more is important. In the longer term you are limiting your earning capacity if you focus only on a salaried job.

To put it in investing terminology, if you're salaried, you have a leverage factor of 1 => the amount you work = a salary of x. More work = more pay.

As you grow older, you gain leverageable assets – your experience and your contacts. You can now work less (relying on your experience and contacts) and earn just as much, or work just as much and earn more, increasing your leverage factor to say 4.

If you start a company, you can pay other people to work for you, and earn you money. This is difficult and fraught with risk, but if you succeed you can increase your leverage to, say, 20. (For each unit of work you get 20x the return, compared to the salary you would earn if you were employed by someone else.)

When your money works for you, you further increase your leverage, sometimes to infinity by living entirely off the return via fixed deposits! (This is no work and plenty of income.)

What I'm saying here is: Focus on increasing your leverage. Whether it is by active investing or working or starting a company, your aim is to build assets (money or business ownership) that can be leveraged.

Essentially get to a stage where you can get your assets working for you, instead of you having to work. This may involve innovative thinking, or simply applying common sense.

Take an example: Doctors apparently have little leverage. They have to work, otherwise they don't get paid. Right? Well, they build certain leverages – specialized degrees, experience and fame – and eventually get to a point where they earn more. For instance, neurosurgeons get paid more than GPs.

To further leverage, they might build a nursing home, or a hospital, or set up a pathology lab or even launch a pharmaceuticals company. (There's Dr Trehan, Dr Devi Shetty, Dr Lal, Dr Reddy of Apollo and many other examples.) Owning a hospital means that when you get old and your hands are shaky, you're still earning an income.

If you're not a doctor, don't get depressed (or you'll need one!). You can still create assets. For one, active investing can speed up the process if you're good at this. Active investing means identifying and investing in companies that beat the indices, tracking your own investments and protecting your capital from losses.

One interesting point: The more leverage you have, the less taxes you pay as a percentage of income.
- Salary income carries the highest tax: The highest tax bracket is 43 per cent with very few deductions
- Business income (consultancy, etc.) still has 30 per cent to 43 per cent as the highest bracket, but you can deduct depreciation on your car, phone expenses, travel expenses etc
- If you start a company, you'll pay as little as 25 per cent taxes.
- For stock market investments the long-term gains are taxed at 10 per cent

Yes, tax rates will change but this trend remains true, not just in India but everywhere. Equity investments are always taxed at lower rates than corporate profits, which in turn are taxed at lower rates than consulting income, and salaries.

'Where's your Ferrari?'

The story goes that a reporter was talking to a woman, who was smoking a cigarette.

'Do you smoke a lot?' asks the reporter.

'Well, two packs a day,' says the woman, puffing away.

'And for how many years, if I may ask?'

'Twenty-five years, and I know I should stop,' says the woman.

'That's twenty-five years at 40 cigarettes a day,' says the reporter. 'At Rs 10 per cigarette, that's Rs 400 a day, or Rs 146,000 a year for 25 years. If you had saved that money and invested it in the stock market instead, you would have had Rs 3 crore by now!'

'See how bad smoking is for you? That's enough money to buy a Ferrari!' he continues.

The woman thinks about this. She stubs out the cigarette slowly, and asks, 'Aha. Do you smoke, sir?'

'Of course not!' he says.

'So,' she continues, throwing the stub into a garbage can, 'where's your Ferrari?'

This seems like just a funny story but it also has an important lesson. We know how compounding works. Take Rs 100 and at 10 per cent, it will double in 7 years. It will, indeed, but only if you actually save the Rs 100. If you only focus on the math, there's no point giving sermons about how rich you would be, if you did.

Returns matter but not as much as the saving habit. Take two people. Anjaan and Sumit. Anjaan saves Rs 10,000 a month for 10 years and invests in stocks.

Sumit saves the same Rs 10,000 a month. But he invests in a less aggressive bond fund, increasing his contribution by 10 per cent every year. Just a slight increase, you think.

	Anjaan	Sumit
Invests	Rs 10,000 a month	Rs 10,000 a month Increasing at 10 per cent a year
For	10 years	10 years
Where?	Stock market	Boring bond fund
How much does he make?	15 per cent a year (wow)	8 per cent a year
Ends up with	Rs 27.5 lakh	Rs 29.2 lakh

What? Sumit ended up with more money? You can tell me that oh, Anjaan invested quite a bit less. Yes, he did. He invested Rs 12 lakh. And Sumit invested Rs 20 lakh.

But you forget something. Both invest and then the rest of their money would just get spent. A little here, a little there, you don't even notice it, and it's gone.

Anjaan invested a little less than Sumit every year. Sumit invested 10 per cent more each year even though he invested in something that gave him just about half the return Anjaan got, because Sumit wanted peace of mind.

Stock markets – fun, but scary. Fixed income, boring but reliable.

And yet, because of a little extra saving, the boring fixed income beat the fun stock market.

Clearly, saving a little more has a greater impact on your returns, in the long run, than simply finding that fantastic stock, or bond, or mutual fund. People focus too much on the latter aspect. It's the former – saving more – that has a greater impact on long-term goals.

The saying goes: If you have an hour to cut a tree, you should spend 50 minutes sharpening the axe. But it's boring!

How to deal with lack of excitement

You know investing is boring, but you have to have some fun. Especially when everyone's laughing all the way to the bank. (This saying doesn't apply in India's traffic, btw. No matter how much money you make, you're going to be cursing all the way. But we digress.)

So, what I suggest is: Carve out a little amount to play with in markets and have some fun. This should be less than 5 per cent of your money. Just use that as a sandbox to do things that sound interesting. Buying a stock. That new IPO. Some 'futures and options'. It's an education, and it's a source of entertainment. But it's probably not going to enrich your life meaningfully in monetary terms, at least not at first.

You can think of it as a fun thing to do, like going to the movies or dining out at a fancy restaurant. But the lessons you learn from such a sandbox are far more valuable than the fees you pay in college. You learn from the school of hard knocks and that's a degree more valuable than all the other degrees you've ever gotten.

Getting back to business

This is so boring, Deepak! Tell me the juicy stuff. I hear you. I know it's boring. This comes from a person who has seen how exciting the stock market is. And heard how easy it is to believe that money will just multiply if you invest in stocks. The narrative is that things will keep happening every day and you'll just get rich quickly.

The 'rich-o-fication' happens slowly. While you sleep. And more money is made sitting and waiting, than buying or selling. But you've got your little sandbox. Stock markets, ahoy!

Before we get there, we have to be sure you're all set when it comes to the basics – emergency funds and so on.

The basics: Your emergency fund and insurance

Before we delve into the complexities of investing, we're going to look at the very basic things that this book will not cover. In the pecking order of things, there are a few 'hygiene' elements that are absolutely must.

If you don't have these, don't read the rest of this book. This is really important.

First, you need an emergency fund. This is a fund that meets your expenses for about six months. Not income, expenses. Because many of you are earning enough to save gazillions of money, and others aren't earning quite enough every month (but there's a bonanza once in a while). Mark your expenses, multiply that monthly number by 6 and please focus on ensuring you have that first.

Once you have that, park it in liquid funds or fixed deposits. Put it in a place that you can withdraw cash from within 24 hours. Do not consider this money part of your net worth any more.

Some banks provide fixed deposits that are 'linked' to your savings account. So just create such a linked fixed deposit and any time you go below zero-balance while, say, paying a hospital bill, the bank will automatically draw money out from your fixed deposit.

You will use this money in an emergency. When you don't have a job, or you're injured or out of action at any point. This is absolutely important; use this money then, and when you're back in action, refill this emergency fund to take it back to six months of expenses.

If you don't have enough for an emergency fund, you're in deep, deep, trouble and should not be investing in anything else.

Think about this another way: When is an emergency? It may be yours personally, like if you had an accident. But it's more likely to be if you've lost a job. And that could be because the economy is in bad shape. And if that's the case, the stock market isn't doing so well. If you draw money from your stock market investments when the markets are not doing well, you're effectively losing a lot of money, even if you get back on your feet within, say, six months.

The stock market sees a correction often. And if the market recovers, say, 20 per cent in the next six months, you have effectively paid a fee of 20 per cent to take your money out from stocks and put it back in after six months. An emergency fund saves that cost – even if your money isn't entirely invested. Focusing on lost opportunity is a bad idea here – it takes away from the security the emergency fund offers you. Effectively, not having an emergency fund is like a car driver refusing to wear a seat belt because it feels less comfortable.

Life insurance: This is a complex beast. Let's only talk about term insurance, where you don't get any money back if you survive. Because everyone tells you that you must have insurance. But it's not always true.

Insurance is simply this: *If I die, does someone who depends on me have the money to survive the rest of their life?*

Take Aarav Bhandari. He's forty years old and he's got Rs 20 lakh as savings. His wife, Tanya, works for a salary of Rs 25,000 a month as a teacher. His five-year-old daughter, Amaya, will start school next year.

He makes a salary of Rs 1,00,000 a month, and they spend about Rs 50,000 a month overall, rent and household expenses and all that. Tanya is speaking with him about insurance.

'We only have twenty lakh rupees. Look, it's not like you're going to die, but apparently we do need to talk about this insurance thing.'

'What do you think we need?' asks Aarav. Because he has no idea.

Tanya starts thinking. 'Listen, if you aren't around, I'm going to be heartbroken and I'll have to parent Amaya alone. We'll have to get this fifty thousand rupees a month from somewhere and the ten lakh rupees we have will last us forty months. That's it. Obviously we need to cover for more.'

She goes on. 'So obviously we need to generate fifty thousand rupees a month, or six lakh rupees a year. The simple thing would be to say if we had one crore rupees, we could put it in a long-term fixed deposit at 6 per cent and get six lakh rupees a year.'

'But costs go up due to inflation, no?' says Aarav.

Tanya carries on. 'We've seen our costs go up 5 per cent a year. So in year two, we'll spend six lakh thirty thousand and so on. In fourteen years our expenses double. In thirty years we're going to need to spend thirty lakh rupees a year! We need a corpus that generates this growing requirement – for another, say, fifty years. This adds up to . . . let me do this on a spreadsheet . . . okay, Rs 12.5 crore.'

Aarav is fascinated, and worried. *Do I need to start gambling?* 'Maybe one crore rupees isn't right, but Rs 12.5 crore isn't right either, no? Isn't there a decent middle ground?'

'Good point. Mathematically, I'll take the assumption that we can get a return of 6 per cent a year. There's this complex formula, which tells me the actual number is around Rs 2.3 crore. If I plug that in with this concept: I start spending six lakh rupees a year, which increases at 5 per cent every year, for fifty years. Plug that into this formula, and we get a rough figure of Rs 2.3 crore to start with.'

'I won't ask you how it works, but what does this do?'

'Every year, I generate 6 per cent returns. In the first year, I earn Rs 13.8 lakh as a return on that corpus. I only spend six lakh rupees. That's Rs 7.8 lakh left that goes back into the corpus. The next year I have to spend Rs 6.3 lakh, but I generate Rs 14.3 lakh (since my corpus actually went up!). Again, I feed back the excess into the corpus. This keeps going on until eventually the inflation makes my monthly spend so much that my returns can't meet it – and I withdraw from the base corpus. Eventually, in fifty years, I go to zero.'

Take a look at the attached table and graphs to understand what Tanya is talking about. We've shown the first eight years and the last eight in the table. Assume they start saving at age forty, and spend more only as they grow older. The graphs show how savings peak around age seventy-two, and then expenses mount.

Age	Start of year	Return at 6 per cent p.a.	Expenses increase at 5 per cent p.a.	Savings end of year
40	2,30,00,000	13,80,000	6,00,000	2,37,80,000
41	2,37,80,000	14,26,800	6,30,000	2,45,76,800
42	2,45,76,800	14,74,608	6,61,500	2,53,89,908
43	2,53,89,908	15,23,394	6,94,575	2,62,18,727
44	2,62,18,727	15,73,124	7,29,304	2,70,62,547
45	2,70,62,547	16,23,753	7,65,769	2,79,20,531
46	2,79,20,531	16,75,232	8,04,057	2,87,91,706
47	2,87,91,706	17,27,502	8,44,260	2,96,74,948
...	...	...	...	...
...	...	...	...	...
84	3,29,66,186	19,77,971	51,34,290	2,98,09,867
85	2,98,09,867	17,88,592	53,91,005	2,62,07,454
86	2,62,07,454	15,72,447	56,60,555	2,21,19,347

contd...

...contd

Age	Start of year	Return at 6 per cent p.a.	Expenses increase at 5 per cent p.a.	Savings end of year
87	2,21,19,347	13,27,161	59,43,583	1,75,02,925
88	1,75,02,925	10,50,175	62,40,762	1,23,12,339
89	1,23,12,339	7,38,740	65,52,800	64,98,279
90	64,98,279	3,89,897	68,80,440	7,736

'You're out of money in fifty years? That would be rough,' says Aarav.

'Yes, but you have to stop planning somewhere. We can round it up to Rs 2.5 crore and leave a little more for extras,' says Tanya. 'But we have twenty lakh rupees already, so the insurance we need is ...'

'... Rs 2.3 crore!' exclaims Aarav. 'I wonder what that will cost ... let me check. This insurance website says that if you're forty and a non-smoker, you'll be able to buy a Rs 2.4 crore policy for

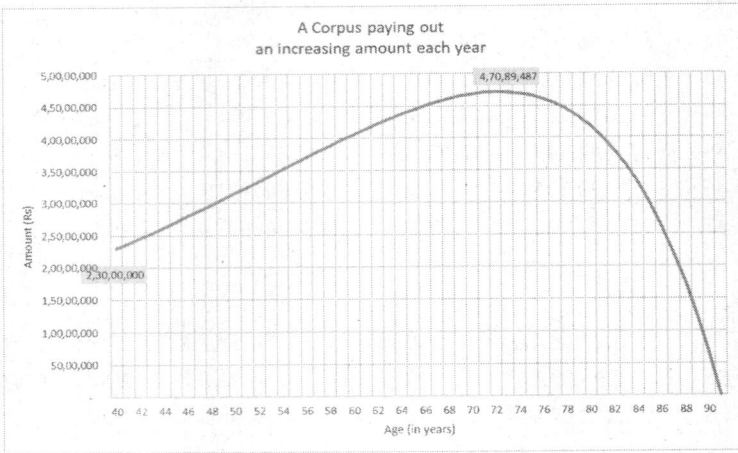

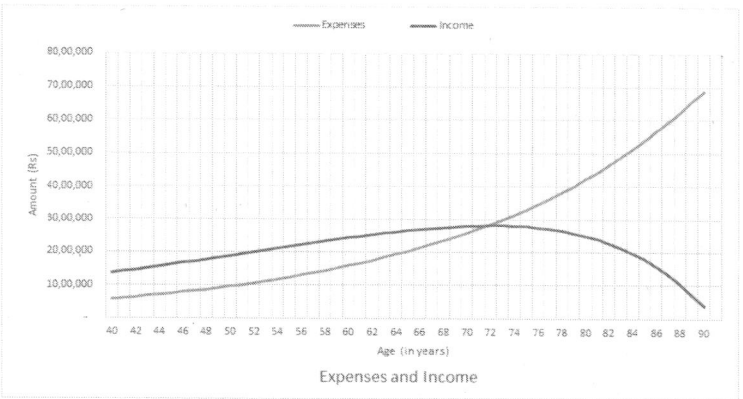

Expenses and Income

Rs 37,000 a year. This is about three thousand rupees month, which we can easily afford,' he continues.

Tanya's a little worried. Is that enough? She realizes why it's not. 'Wait, what about Amaya's graduate education?'

Aarav thinks carefully. 'We could bump this up to three crore rupees instead. I'm sure the excess fifty lakh rupees, at 6 per cent growth, in thirteen years when she turns eighteen, will end up as . . .'

'. . . 1 crore,' says Tanya. 'That should pay for most of it, assuming college costs forty lakh rupees for four years today, even with inflation.'

While Tanya's calculating this, Aarav looks at having a 3 crore insurance. For his age (40), it's about Rs 3700 a month. Not unaffordable.

Tanya thinks further. 'But if we invest our savings now, and get a decent return, it's possible that in ten years, we will see our savings grow to more than a crore! Isn't that something to think about?'

'We'll just redo the calculations then!' says Aarav.

This story is an example of a couple that needs insurance. You can use similar logic to figure it out for yourself.

But there are quite a few instances during your life journey when you *don't* need insurance.

- You're fresh out of college. No dependants. If you die, people will be sad. But no one will be financially in danger. You don't need insurance.
- Your children have grown up and don't depend on you for income. You need no insurance. You have no loans, and have enough to last you for the rest of your life.
- You're rich enough already. (Imagine Tanya already having Rs 3 crore in her bank account.) No need for life insurance.

Now, when you buy insurance, just buy term insurance with no money back if you survive. That's the simplest cheapest solution. Everything else will cost too much, so you'll buy too little of it and be under-insured. Which is a terrible thing.

Why, you think? Why can't I take a policy where, if I survive, I get my money back? There are such policies, but they offer you a big problem – not enough insurance. Consider a policy which paid back all the premium if the person survived. This would cost a 40-year-old person, Rs 5,00,000 a year for a Rs 2 crore sum assured. For most people, this becomes unaffordable.

So they do the worst thing – take such a policy but for a lower sum assured. You think, I can only afford Rs 1 lakh a year, so I'll just take a Rs 40 lakh policy. This is equivalent to saying I need to cover my family with fifty years of expenses, but since I really want my money back if I survive, I will only cover them for twelve years instead. Twelve years is hardly enough, and you can't expect them to go looking for other means of survival at that time. Insure what you must have, not less.

Health insurance: Oh, take this for yourself and your family. There's a bunch of things here – family floaters, group insurance (your employer may provide this) and so on. Going into too much detail will need a book of its own, but here's a few tips that might help:
- Many policies have strange restrictions, like they'll pay only Rs 5000 a day for hospitalization. Try to get this as high as possible as rates will go up for sure.
- Buy a base cover that is decent enough to cover for regular hospitalization expenses, as a 'floater' plan (single payment to cover the entire family, for a group amount).
- Then, buy a 'super top up' plan. This is a simple concept – if you get hospitalized and the bill is up to Rs 5 lakh, you pay. Beyond that, the insurer pays. Great for things where you know you're really afraid of that one situation where you get hit with a bill of Rs 50 lakh.
- If you're looking for insurance for your parents, don't add them to your plan. It makes things altogether more expensive. Buy a separate cover for them, which will reduce the overall cost.
- Don't just say you are covered because your company has an insurance plan. If you lose your job, you will lose the insurance as well, and that could be the worst possible time to be not-insured.

But this is all just hygiene.

What about investments? Read on.

MUTUAL FUNDS

Get someone else to do your investing

Mutual fund . . .

'Sahi hai,' says the man on the street. Because they had this massive campaign saying *Mutual Fund Sahi Hai*. The problem isn't that we don't know the answer.

The problem is that we don't know the question. *Sahi* for what? For whom?

'Deepak, dude! What is a mutual fund?'

Now that's a good question.

The logic of buying into mutual funds is simple. As the funds pitch it: Give us your money and we'll manage it for you because you have no idea what to buy to make a profit.

This is actually a sensible pitch, because many of us simply don't have the time. Or the energy, or the skill. Or we just want someone else to do the grunt work for us.

But there can be problems with buying funds as well. Sometimes you will misinterpret the relationship, or the manager will abuse your trust.

These are big words, Deepak. Misinterpret the relationship? Isn't this a weasel way to say they lie to us?

Well, listen, in the finance industry, there is a weasel way to say everything. Nobody ever says, 'You'll lose money'. They say 'risk'. They say 'negative returns'. They will tell you the things they think you want to hear, because deep down most of us have this warm, fuzzy hope that everyone wants to do good things for us.

But sometimes, the funds, or rather, the people who run them, decide to enrich themselves at your expense. Doing good for themselves takes higher priority over doing good to you.

This is what in weasel tongue is called 'a conflict of interest'.

Before you get too cynical about the obvious conflicts of interest, let your inner cynic ask the right questions. And don't let cynicism stop you from being an optimist. If you're going to smell the roses, you're also going to have to learn to avoid the thorns.

Let's dive into why this philosophy of mixing cynicism and optimism applies to mutual funds. But first, a little history. (Warning: Very boring. This is an explanation of all the things mutual funds do and why they do them that way. We've warned you, ok?)

The history of mutual funds: A regulated, pooled investment

Someone long ago bought a lot of shares of different companies. Some of those companies were fraudulent, some others went bust, and the investors lost a lot of money.

So, some people who knew their way around stock markets decided to help people who didn't, by telling them which stocks to buy. For a fee. And this was the birth of the 'Adviser'.

It didn't work that well because some of the clients wouldn't, or couldn't, take the advice. Clients needed to place orders in market hours, when they were busy doing whatever they did to earn a living. Or they were advised to buy at a certain price, but they bought much higher. This even happened sometimes because the adviser was very popular and advising so many people that when all of them bought at the same time, they pushed the prices up. Sometimes people bought the stock a long time after the recommendation, when the story had changed for some reason.

Sometimes, clients would second-guess the adviser and buy only a few stocks and ignore the others. When the ignored stocks shot up, the investors started inventing acronyms like OMG, FOMO and other less mentionable ones.

So even when the adviser was right, many client-investors didn't receive the benefit. So people realized the advisers had time to track the market, figure out new opportunities and so on.

The next step was logical and obvious: Give your adviser the money to manage. It was just easier, and the adviser would execute transactions on your behalf and you didn't face the logistics problems of finding time, or making the effort to call your broker.

This concept expanded into something that's now called a mutual fund. A bunch of investors would pool in money, and a manager would invest the pool. Every day, the pool had a collective value, and each investor held a percentage of that value, based on how much she had invested.

This simple concept led to the first mutual fund. This happened way too long ago, in 1774, in Holland.

The Indian mutual fund story started centuries later, in 1963. The Unit Trust of India (UTI) was formed by the government to do this. UTI would take money from individuals and invest it in stocks. This was supposed to be win-win. Experts would help households invest in profitable businesses, the economy would grow and the government would collect more revenue. But there was a problem with how UTI worked.

The disaster that was US-64 or 'why you can't trust anyone'

In 1964, UTI launched India's first mutual fund scheme, the US-64. This was a huge deal in the sense that people could invest small amounts and still make lots of money. But it was the most horribly run system you could imagine. Or rather, it was run a lot worse than you can probably imagine. What's more, it was a monopoly. No private sector organization was allowed to run a mutual fund. So there was no way to improve things.

The fund bought stocks, but it never revealed how much it bought, or which stocks it owned. UTI would announce an 'NAV' or Net Asset Value every so often – this was a price at which you could buy new units or sell units. (I'll explain what NAV is later – for now, just assume it's the per unit value of a portfolio, net of liabilities.)

But this NAV was apparently a figment of someone's imagination. It turned out there was no relationship between the NAV and the actual underlying valuation of the stocks held by the fund. This was possible largely because regulators were non-existent. Even when SEBI (Securities and Exchange Board of India) was formed much later, in 1992, it was not allowed to regulate UTI. (Now we know why, but at the time it wasn't clear.)

UTI faced competition only in 1987, when SBI (State Bank of India) and Canara Bank were allowed to set up their own mutual fund arms. UTI remained the biggest fund, with over 2 crore investors.

What went wrong?

The fund would regularly declare an NAV that was much higher than the value of the stocks it held. This was fine while there were cash inflows with more and more people looking to invest. Any redemptions of units at NAV could be funded out of the inflows, which were coming to UTI at the same NAV.

But after 1998, the fund saw larger redemptions compared to purchases, which meant that the fund had to pay out net cash at the higher NAV. In 1998, for instance, the NAV per unit was declared to be Rs 14.25 (the price at which you could sell units).* But the underlying valuation of the stocks translated to just Rs 9.68! That meant that the fund was trading units at a far higher price than it could afford. Why would it do that?

This was primarily because of ego. The UTI management didn't want to tell the world that the NAV had fallen because of market conditions. That would make them look bad and incompetent at managing investments. So they did the next best thing: Pretended everything was fine.

Unfortunately for the UTI management, people figured out that it had set the NAV way above intrinsic value. So the redemptions continued to be higher than the inflows.

The government knew this and tried to help. The ethical way to set this right would have been to force UTI to reveal the true NAV. This would have hurt some investors but at least, it would have anchored the fund to some sense of reality. But if you think the government did that, I have a bridge I want to sell you.

Instead, in 1999, the government just decided to buy

---

* https://economictimes.indiatimes.com/us-64-the-myths-reality/articleshow/1024131.cms

truckloads of the stocks UTI owned in this scheme, at roughly double the market valuations. The thinking seemed to be: If you can't bring the NAV down to reality, let's try and bring reality up to the NAV. (This strategy would prove valuable in later years while designing political campaigns on WhatsApp. But we digress.)

This kinda-sorta helped, but then, there was an avalanche in 2001. After the US dotcom bust of 2000 and the Ketan Parekh scam (also 2000), stock valuations plunged 60 per cent. This was horrible and UTI cancelled its dividend because it didn't have the money to pay it.

The government had to step in and 'rescue' the fund. So it offered investors two choices: We'll pay you Rs 12 per unit (or Rs 10 if you have more than 5000 units). Take the money upfront, or take it in the form of a government-guaranteed tax-free bond for five years at 6.75 per cent interest.

In return for the bailout, the government took over all the shares owned by UTI's US-64. The value of those shares at the time was much less than Rs 10 a unit – in fact it was around Rs 5.81.* So it looked like they were doing investors a favour and 'bailing them out'. Investors who exited felt like kings – the government paid over Rs 8500 crore in 2003 for the bailout, and the shares were worth a lot less than that at the time.

The kicker: More than a decade later, the government would end up earning a total return of over Rs 1,00,000 crore from those shares, which included some blue-chip private companies, as well as many duds.

There were many lessons to be learnt from this whole mess.

---

* Rs 5.81 a unit in January 2002: https://www.outlookindia.com/outlookmoney/archive/what-should-us-64-unit-holders-do-now-87387

First, there was a big problem with lack of regulation. UTI wasn't obliged to reveal its portfolio even though it took hard-earned money from investors. We didn't know what the underlying portfolio was, so UTI could release whatever concocted NAV it wanted. That had disastrous consequences. So now, the rule is that mutual funds must reveal their portfolio in full, every month.

Second, we learnt you couldn't 'guarantee' a dividend or return, the way UTI did. This is why mutual funds today can't tell you how much they can give you tomorrow, even if they hold only cash. (Today's NAV is fine. Tomorrow's a no-no. Absolutely no guarantees of any sort can be given about the future.)

Third, investors should probably have refused to take their money back when the government made that offer. Instead, they should have demanded transparency and accepted a lower NAV. (Who am I kidding?) This would have given them much higher returns later. But a chocolate now is better than a chocolate factory later, apparently.

Finally, boring as this history might sound, the saga of UTI is why Indian mutual funds are regulated the way they are. This is why regulators are so careful to outline what mutual funds can and cannot do.

UTI did nasty things – committed outright fraud in fact – and got away clean as an institution. The government did a bailout. Many UTI executives continued to be heavyweights in the finance industry.

The UTI mutual fund continued to exist, but it got smaller and smaller over the years. Private sector mutual funds operate more efficiently and are better at finding investments. So UTI couldn't hold on to market share as the competition heated up.

This experience also led to a certain mindset with regulators: If you can't punish, you will overregulate.

Knowing this history might help you develop a cynical but refreshingly positive attitude as you wade through the rest of this book.

Next let's figure out the following:
- What is a mutual fund?
- All those options in mutual funds: Direct, Regular, Growth, Dividend
- Abeyaar, not just stocks

What is a mutual fund?

Let's say you and I have some money to spare, about 1 lakh each. And we have eight other like-minded friends. We all decide we need to invest in stocks, but we don't have the time, skills or energy to research, track, buy, sell, etc.

So we hire a 'manager' who has the right experience and tell him – look, you can take up to 2.5 per cent of the total value every year as your fees, but your job is to buy shares that will grow over time, and to sell when the time is ripe, etc.

So ten of us have now put in a lakh each, and the total corpus is Rs 10 lakh. We decide that we will issue 'units' to denote our interest in the fund, so we issue 1 lakh units at Rs 10 each. (It's like 'tokens' in a casino, except that you expect to lose money in a casino.) So each person gets 10,000 units, corresponding to an investment of Rs 1 lakh.

The manager we've picked is quite experienced and informed. She makes stock buying decisions based on what we, the investors, decided up front. Her mandate is: Buy only large cap stocks, or technology stocks, and stay at least 90 per cent invested (a maximum of only 10 per cent of the corpus is to be held in cash).

As the value of the stocks held in our portfolio grows, so

does the total corpus value. Let us say the value has gone up to Rs 15.6 lakh in two years. Now, we pay the fund manager 2.5 per cent every year. Let's say that is about Rs 30,000 a year, adding up to Rs 60,000 for two years. So what's left is Rs 15 lakh.

The value of the 1 lakh 'units' is now Rs 15 lakh, meaning each unit is worth Rs 15 – this is the 'Net Asset Value' or the NAV (subtracting liabilities such as salaries and other expenses). Since each of us has 10,000 units, the value of our individual holdings is Rs 1.5 lakh.

What happens when someone sells?

Now I decide to take a trip to Singapore and budget to spend Rs 75,000. So I 'sell' or 'redeem' half my units at the current NAV, meaning I sell 5000 units at Rs 15. To give me the money, the fund manager sells some stocks, and now the 'total corpus' is reduced to Rs 14.25 lakh.

That will again grow with time, but I will personally see lower returns than you, because I have only 5000 units and you have 10,000.

Same fund – another common 'use case'

One day, when the NAV is Rs 15 per unit, the fund manager decides the market is going to fall. So she sells half the holdings. Now there is half the money in stocks and half the money in the bank as cash. Now she's supposed to keep a maximum of 10 per cent in cash, but there aren't any opportunities worth pursuing at that moment. So the manager gives us the money as a 'dividend'. Let's say she decides to give us Rs 5 per unit as a dividend, for 1 lakh units (ignore the selling in the above example – this is a different example of what can happen in a fund).

You get Rs 50,000 as dividend. But the total corpus has fallen by Rs 5 lakh. So the NAV (total corpus divided by number of units) is going to fall by Rs 5 per unit. So a dividend pay-out for a mutual fund is the same as no dividend – you get some money, but your fund value goes down by the same amount.

Note: This is why mutual funds that distribute dividend are now called 'Transfer of Income Distribution cum Capital Withdrawal Plan'. The name was selected by a complex procedure involving a game of scrabble.

This is how a mutual fund operates. Now, funds can be misused (managers can run away, etc.). So the government has very strict regulations for organized mutual funds. They must have a sponsor (usually a bank), a set of trustees (some of whom are independent persons), and an asset management company (AMC) that runs each mutual fund through a fund manager who works for the AMC.

Every fund has to publish a clear mandate that defines the types and sizes of stocks and other assets it can buy and hold, the maximum it can hold in cash or non-core assets, etc. It has to declare its NAV daily, and it has to allow redemption at that NAV. Every AMC can have only one fund for one type of investment, which means only one large-cap equity fund, one small-cap equity fund, etc.

Evolution: A simple strategy to make money with mutual funds

Let's assume you've chosen the right sort of manager, and she invests in the right sort of things – stocks, gold, bonds, whatever, and you make money. There's thousands of funds and schemes out there.

When you first think about investing in a fund, you literally don't know where to start making choices.

Let's think of how people start.

First, you start by trying to feel smart.

Many websites out there rank mutual funds based on 'performance'. How well has a fund done in the recent past? Take these funds and rank them all by one year returns and choose maybe the top two or three.

Very quickly, you realize this is a losing strategy. You've just selected a fund that got supremely lucky, and after you got in, you see that the subsequent-year fund performance has been terrible! What's wrong?

You talk to a friend. 'Dude, I chose the RMS Banking Fund and PDFC Top 100 Fund. [NB: These aren't real names, at the time of writing at least.] They're both sucking on returns! Why?'

'Abeyaar, RMS Banking Fund has like 1 crore in AUM.'

He's getting all Buddhist on me, you think. AUM and all. 'What?' you exclaim loudly, hoping for more information.

'AUM. Assets Under Management. How much money the fund has. Rs 1 crore is like nothing. There's no point going with tiny funds, where the manager can't even justify a salary at his one per cent fees. At least 100 crore or more, please.'

'Okay, but this PDFC Top 100 is like, oh my goodness, Rs 15,000 crore. That should be enough, no?' you ask.

'Yes, but it seems like this fund is only decent in the one year time frame. Take two years, or three, or four, and it's at the bottom of the ranking list.'

Now you're getting it. We need the funds that rank well in the three year and five year time frames. Not just the one year.

Alphabet Soup

You're now a little more knowledgeable. So you go in to find the best funds that have done excellently in three and five years as well. You select the top four. Let's call them A, B, C and D.

After a year, you do this again, and voila, the top four list is different. It's A, X, Y, Z.

What's a person to do? You say, well, let me keep investing in A, X, Y and Z and stop investing in B, C and D. Phew.

Within four years, you own 15 funds. It's an alphabet soup. You've consistently invested Rs 10,000 a month, which has become a decent Rs 7 lakh. But you have no idea why the best funds keep changing positions!

Why not sell the weakest and buy the strongest only? Because every year you'll end up selling and paying taxes. Argh, you think. Give 10 per cent of my returns to the government? Why?

You find an online website that does 'mutual fund analysis'. You input your data. It tells you that 12 of your 15 funds have a very large number of common stocks.

You think about this a little. *You were smart.* You started by picking the best performers. In a few years, the best performers changed. You changed alongside. You did everything right. And yet, you're struggling with one thing you have no idea about:

> *Is my smartness contributing anything to my returns? Could I have just stuck with the first few funds and made just as much?*

You're going to need help, you think.

Get yourself some advice

Someone puts you in touch with this guy who's a mutual fund guru. You talk to him. He's willing to help you, for free!

You show him your list of mutual funds. He shakes his head. Not because he's stunned. Because he's seen it before. The rankers. The hodgepodge. These funds, he tells you, are useless.

'I have better funds. You should consider my funds instead,' he says.

'But what do I do with my 15 funds?' you ask.

'Er, let me rank them by performance. Keep the top seven, sell the bottom eight, and reinvest that money in my four funds.' His approach seems fine, and maybe having only 11 funds is better than 15.

You go ahead, still wondering why someone would do this for free. The next year, he comes back to you again.

'Here, I've ranked all the 11 funds as investments again,' he says. 'Why don't we sell the bottom six, and buy these other four funds I now like?'

You stare at him. 'Wait, you had different funds last year,' you say.

'That's because the fund performance has moved from [the Guru spouts some random jargon] to [some more jargon], so we should shift.'

At this point, you have to ask. 'Why are you doing this for free?'

'Oh, I do get paid, as commissions from the funds,' he says.

You're okay with paying. But is this really necessary, because he's doing exactly what you were doing – ranking, rebalancing, finding new funds? You still hold a lot of funds, and they're still all buying similar things.

ABC small-cap fund, you check, has HDFC Bank – which is one of the top five stocks in India. HDFC Bank is also there in XYZ large-cap fund. And in PQR flexi cap fund. Why are they all buying the same thing? Can I just buy one fund instead? Should I?

There's such a thing as too much diversification, without getting any real diversification. If HDFC Bank falls 5 per cent, your large cap fund falls. Your small cap fund also falls. This is stupid, because they're supposed to be independent. But they've both invested in the same company!

So having 11 funds is a bad idea, you might think. What do you really want?

I just need something that's usually in the top 25 per cent of funds, dammit. I don't care about the top four – just do decently well, please, in comparison with the others. Is there a secret?

The adviser is helpful. You don't realize the holdings are ephemeral, he tells you. 'They might hold HDFC Bank today, but the manager may sell it tomorrow. Let's just let the fund manager do his thing – after all, you're paying for them to perform, and then you question the way they do it?'

This reminds you of a movie that includes the line, 'You can't handle the truth.' So you find yourself another adviser.

Who tells you that these funds are okay, but here, I have four shiny new funds that have done better.

And then you discover a little secret that no one tells you about because, hey, there are no commissions for telling you about this.

The index fund

We have something called the BSE Sensex and something called the NSE Nifty. These are indices – groups of stocks, which contain the top stocks of each stock exchange. Each stock has a weight in the index – HDFC Bank may be 5 per cent of it, while JSW Steel may be 1 per cent. The weights change over time since this depends on the market capitalization, and stocks may come in, or go out, of the indices.

You can't buy a portfolio of 30 or 50 separate stocks. But if you have a fund that matches the index, you should get the Nifty or Sensex returns over time. So, why not just buy those stocks as a group if you can?

Look deeper and you find that most mutual funds struggle to beat the Nifty. And no matter when you look, the Nifty index always seems to be consistently among the top performers.

An index mutual fund is simply a fund that follows an index. What if a mutual fund just invested in the top 100 stocks as reflected by the Nifty 100 index? If you bought that fund alone, you are likely to be in the top performing funds.

There are several reasons why index funds do well: Low fees, for one. Fees are typically linked to high fund manager salaries, a research team, etc. With an active mutual fund, you'll need research analysts to draw up projections, talk to management, get street feedback about a company, etc. With an index fund, you have no such need. You just invest in the index companies. The fund doesn't have a choice because that's what the mandate is. This reduces fund management fees.

A typical fund that charges 1 per cent asset management fees will earn Rs 10 crore when it has Rs 1000 crore under management. This pays for all the salaries. Given lower staffing needs, an index fund that has Rs 1000 crore AUM might only charge Rs 2 crore as fees – which is 0.2 per cent.

So if the index goes up 15 per cent in a year, you'll make 14.8 per cent in the index fund. But the active fund will have to make 15.8 per cent, and then charge 1 per cent fees, just to keep pace with the index fund. This is a challenge only top funds can meet – and the composition of funds that make the cadre of 'top' funds will change every year, since a fund may do well in one year and not so well in the next.

This is why your ranking of funds and investing in them every year resulted in so many different funds. And this is also why just having an index fund may be better, and less cumbersome, than choosing a new fund each year.

But with only 0.2 per cent expense ratios, there's no room for commissions. So, no one pitches index funds to you.

Also, it's ego-threatening to recommend an index fund. How dare you tell me I can't do better than the average? It's like telling me I'm a bad driver – even if I have three accidents a year. This statement hurts anyone who believes he's intelligent enough to beat the index – and advisers have to prove they can, in order to justify their fees.

But then, think of it this way. The 'average' index is better than most mutual funds every year. It's already above average in performance since by definition it contains the market leaders. You're just sticking with the winners, by definition.

A stock that's big enough to be in the Nifty is in your fund. If it's not big enough, or loses its mojo, the exchange takes it out of the index, and replaces it. And by definition, you own the replacement too, because your index fund will mirror the exchange and make the same replacement. You're always connected with the top companies. If you really want to be with the top, then be with the top.

Beyond the index fund is a three-letter acronym you'll hear more often: The ETF or Exchange Traded Fund is an index fund that's traded on a stock exchange. Instead of buying directly from the mutual fund. Wait, I hear you think: What's the difference between an index fund and an ETF?

The ETF is just an index fund packaged to be sold on the stock exchange. You can buy units directly on the exchange, from other people who want to sell. This is different from a mutual fund which you transact (buy or sell) only with the AMC itself. The AMC will release an NAV every day, even for an ETF, but to buy directly from it you may need a substantial amount of money. A Nifty ETF, for instance, might set a minimum threshold of about 75 lakh rupees (and multiples of that) for direct transaction with the AMC. You want smaller amounts? Buy on the stock exchange instead.

ETFs are immensely popular in the US, where they offer a significant set of tax advantages to retail investors. Basically, buying and selling an index fund sees a higher tax hit in America than buying and selling an ETF. Plus, in the US, mutual funds ask for minimum investments of $2500 or more, while ETFs are far lower in value.

In India, the differences are not so acute. The ETF has no tax advantage. The minimum transactions in Indian mutual funds can be as low as Rs 500. And ETFs can cost a lot more, since in the market the ETF can trade at a price that's higher than its NAV itself, and then there are the costs of brokerage and exchange charges.

I'll add a layer more on top of this logic. The best companies in the world are not in India. Apple, Microsoft, Amazon, etc. are listed in the US. You might want to add an international index, such as Nasdaq100, to the mix. There are mutual funds that allow you to access the international indices, relatively cheaply. Plus, this would give you a hedge against the rupee getting weaker because you own a dollar asset and, over time, the rupee has gotten consistently weaker.

So you could do a mix of the two – Indian and US indexes – as a strategy.

This is a simple concept, but even a 50:50 Indian Index–US Index combination has beaten nearly all of the biggest mutual funds in India, since 2018. The year 2018 was a game changer for mutual funds since SEBI decided exactly how certain funds could invest. All fund returns after that have been limited by these restrictions.

So the secret sauce is:
- A Nifty Index Fund
- An international index fund

For the equity portion of your allocation, this is 'risk'. For a lower risk component, we could go into fixed income funds. But mutual funds are like stock market investments, no? No.

Abeyaar, it's not just about stocks

'I just bought a mutual fund,' said Anita, looking at Ravi. 'We've got to invest, and I'm putting away something every month for Anand's education.'

'He's three!' Ravi said, looking at the little fellow who would pronounce it 'free years old', which was philosophically correct.

'So I'm going to wait till he's seventeen?' said Anita, with a twinkle in her eye. Ravi, like her, was an engineer, but he just didn't get the concept of compounding. She'd have to explain it to him.

'But mutual funds are risky, baba! How many times have I told you that the stock markets are all frauds and you'll lose all our money?' exclaimed Ravi, happy that the WhatsApp community had given him enough ammunition.

He had his own sob story too. Of how he invested in this Rs 2 stock thinking he could only lose Rs 2, and then he actually lost it all, an amount considerably higher than Rs 2 because he bought 100,000 shares. Somehow this didn't make sense. So the way he looked at it, the stock market consisted of a bunch of scamsters waiting in ambush to take his money.

Anita sighed. That Rs 2 story again, she thought. 'Ravi, just because you buy some silly penny stock your uncle told you about, doesn't mean anything, no? And then, how do you know I've invested in stocks?'

'But, you said . . . mutual fund, no?'

'Yes, but why does that have to be stocks?'

'Dudette,' said Ravi, getting into mansplaining mode. 'Mutual funds buy stocks, ya. That's what they do.'

'Abeyaar,' sighed Anita, exasperated. It wasn't just the lack of knowledge. It was the attitude – or indeed, the lack of the right kind. 'Mutual funds can buy a lot of things, not just stocks. Who told you they're only for stocks? Listen to me and I'll explain like you're two years older than Anand.'

She continued, 'Ravi, mutual funds can buy a lot of things. Stocks. Bonds. Fixed deposit–type things. Gold. Gold-backed bonds. And even strange beasts they call Repo and OIS and all that.'

'What? But all of that is risky!'

'Only if you drink too much . . . aw, forget the rhymes. Of course, everything is risky at some level, but there's different layers to it. Your bank deposit sounds safe, but what if your bank goes bust? The guarantee of any deposit is only till five lakh rupees and then you could lose the rest. Mutual funds can buy lots of things that are safer than stocks.'

'Like what?'

'Like if you give the government money for three months for a small amount of interest, what are the chances of losing money in three months?'

'Our government? Dudette, they'll print the rupees and give it back if they don't have it! That's like super safe.' Ravi was excited – could you actually give the government money that they will pay back? It was a one-way street, always, in his mind.

'Yeah, but in the middle – say in one and a half months – the market can pay a slightly different price for this three-month loan, and you might see some fluctuations in price up and down. However, in three months, you're okay. So there's some intermediate risk, but it gets less over time and at the three-month period, you're okay. Think of a mutual fund that only lends for three months at a time, to the government.'

'Okay, that's not bad, that's kinda safe, you would think.'

'Maybe it also lends a little to state governments but for three months or less. Or to public sector companies, again, for three months or less.'

'What kind of public sector companies?' asked Ravi.

'Oh you know, public sector banks, the likes of NTPC, and such things.'

'That's safe, at least in my mind. But you're right, some intermediate pricing risk may be there. In a three-month period that should be okay.'

'Imagine a mutual fund that mixes only such three-month lending,' said Anita, 'with maybe some big corporates like Reliance thrown in.'

'What's the point, though? Won't a fixed deposit be higher in interest rates?' asked Ravi. Safe had to mean lower interest rates, in his head.

'Oh it doesn't have to be!' said Anita. 'For many years, such funds – called liquid funds – have given higher returns than fixed deposits. And remember, a fixed deposit gives interest that is taxed. I could keep money in a liquid fund for years and not pay any taxes till I sell. And right now, I want to save, not sell.'

'This is cool,' said Ravi. 'Low risk, and better taxation than fixed deposits. So mutual funds can do this too? What else?'

'What if I said **one year** instead of three months? Would that scare you? But no equity – just bonds, which is like a security that pays interest?'

Ravi sat down and thought. 'Of course, if the interest rate is higher you could invest in these types of funds with one-year bonds too. Sounds less safe than three months, but if you are speaking of PSUs, and government and big corporates only, then it might still be safer than equity.'

Finally, thought Anita, he's getting it.

'Now I'll throw you a math question. I put one-third my money in the three-month exposure fund, one-third in a one-year exposure, and one-third in a ten-year fund. How risky is that?'

Mind-blowing, thought Ravi. He was in awe of Anita anyhow. But this was a different level altogether.

'Amazing! And without equity!' said Ravi aloud. 'You could keep investing in such a combination for a long time and its tax efficient because you're not selling!'

'Good point, plus all I'm doing is a combination of three funds doing slightly different things. One's a liquid fund, one is a low-duration fund, and the third is a gilt fund. Together, they lend to different types of companies/government/banks and I feel like unless the entire system collapses, I'll be okay.'

Ravi was now perplexed. 'Wait, couldn't you also add equity to this, say, one-fourth of the total fund, and get some more returns?'

'Now you're talking!' said Anita. 'That's my plan after six months. Build a little kitty of safety so that I don't feel miserable, and then add equity to the mix. Risk can grow on you!'

Like you have, thought Ravi. But that would unnecessarily disrupt the flow. And he was curious.

'You said gold too? There's funds that own gold?'

'Yes, and instead of having to deal with having gold at our house, and because we only care about how it adds another dimension to our savings, we can buy a gold mutual fund instead.'

'Add that to the mix!' shouted Ravi. 'But doesn't it get too much? What else could you add?'

'As long as they're not all doing the same thing, we're fine. Different things and we get to diversify too – so when equity markets are down, gold is up, etc. We could add international stocks. We could add real estate investment trusts, and power transmission lines and all sorts of mutualized investments.'

'So mutual funds aren't just about stocks, Ravi,' said Anita. 'There's more money in non-equity funds – liquids, short-term and long-term debt schemes – than in equity. You just heard stocks because that's what you've been conditioned to hear. You've gotta stop hearing and start listening.' She smiled.

Her lips are moving, but I'm not sure I know what she's talking about, thought Ravi. But then, I'm so glad she's on top of this stuff, and maybe I should just pile on.

'Take my money too? I seem to do really stupid things with it, so why don't we save for Anand together?' said Ravi. 'After all, it's not all stocks, and it's diversified enough so we can't lose all of it! How has this done in the past?'

'Dude,' said Anita, countering the -ette, 'investing in liquid and bond funds in the last ten years has given nearly as much of a return as equity funds. Circle of life. Sometimes you have to do the stuff that doesn't look at all exciting, and do it long enough for it to be worthwhile.'

'Kinda like parenting,' he murmured.

This conversation simplifies what mutual funds might do, but they can do a whole lot of things. Here's a list:

Equity funds: Invest in stocks

- Large-cap funds: We're going to invest in the largest 100 companies for the most part. Largest in terms of market capitalization, meaning what you would get if every single share of the company was sold at that price on that day.
- Mid-cap funds: Okay, we'll go slightly lower. Stocks 101 to 250, in terms of size.
- Small-cap funds: We love to inflict pain on ourselves, so we'll scrape the bottom of the barrel. Potentially huge returns but also big risks.
- Large- and mid-cap funds: Tell me you're cheating. Which one are you? (Both, they answer.)
- Multi-cap funds: We can do a little bit of everything. But we'll have everything, from pickle to main course to dessert.
- Flexi-cap funds: We can buy whatever we want, okay?

Debt funds: Invest in fixed income

- Overnight funds: Invest in stuff that if you put money and take it out tomorrow, you're unlikely to lose money. Very complex stuff, which is mostly interbank instruments.
- Liquid funds: Buy bonds that 'mature' in three months or less.
- Ultra-short-term, low duration and short-term funds: Fancy names for funds that buy fixed income securities targeted to mature between three months and three years.
- PSU and banking debt funds: Give loans to the public sector, or banks only.
- Gilt funds: The government is your best friend if you're a Gilt fund, and you aren't allowed to have any other best friends.
- Dynamic bond funds, corporate bond funds: You already hate this book, don't you?
- Credit risk funds: Just invest in equity, yaar. Really high-risk stuff that Nobel Prize winners lose money in!

Hybrid funds

- We're going to cheat and do a bit of the debt thing and a bit of the equity thing and call it aggressive hybrid and conservative hybrid and all that.
- Why? We can charge higher fees than doing them separately. But there's a better explanation: Sometimes it helps keep things simple. A 20 per cent equity, 80 per cent debt fund might be the right fit as a single product for someone who doesn't want too much of an equity exposure, but not too little either. The long-term returns of these funds tend to beat fixed deposit returns without adding substantial risk.
- Arbitrage funds: A special kind of tax-protected fund that invests in equity stocks, but also goes 'short' (sells the stock

with a contract that settles on a future date). This provides low-risk arbitrage, and the returns tend to be the same as debt funds of the liquid or ultra-short-term sort. The tax advantage is that you get taxed on these funds as if they were equity funds, which is far lower than taxation on debt funds.

Fund names can be confusing, so don't buy by looking at the name alone. A fund might call itself the 'XYZ savings fund', but it doesn't behave like a savings account and actually invests in equity. You have to look at the category of the fund and the kind of stocks one is allowed to invest in. Additionally, you're going to need to check if the fund actually buys in accordance with the mandate. If the largest holding in a small-cap fund is HDFC Bank (which is among the three largest and most valuable Indian stocks), you know there's something wrong with this story. The fund has just become an 'index hugger', a term that indicates when a manager simply buys the top index stocks in large quantities just so that his fund can keep pace with the index.

Remember also that there's usually a direct proportion between risk and reward. That means this: The higher the reward, the higher the risk is expected to be. A case in point here was the massive saga of Franklin.

The Franklin saga

Franklin Templeton India has run a successful mutual fund house for decades. Their debt funds were known to deliver the best returns in the market. When all other debt funds struggled to get 7 per cent, Franklin's debt funds would give 9 per cent. Investors loved them, because they managed things very well. Until April 2020.

The reason Franklin was able to get better returns on debt was that they were willing to buy bonds other fund houses refused to touch. Some of the bonds were from companies that didn't have the most pristine of balance sheets. Some others were backed entirely by shares of public companies, exposing the fund to sudden drops in underlying share prices.

A messy situation in 2019 saw the price of Zee Entertainment shares tank precipitously in a short period. Why would this impact a Franklin debt fund? Debt funds buy debt, not equity.

But in this case, there was a peculiar hidden link. The promoters of Zee, the Subhash Chandra family, had pledged their Zee shares against money they had borrowed through bonds. The buyers of these bonds included Franklin (and, to be fair, Aditya Birla Sun Life Mutual Fund and HDFC Mutual Fund as well). When the prices of the shares fell, the promoter entity bonds did not have sufficient collateral, or sufficient cash flows of their own, to repay those bonds. This was resolved with a bond restructure, but the seeds of doubt had been sown – are these debt funds really safe?

In April 2020, after Covid-19 had caused the whole world to start locking down, Franklin's funds were seeing strong redemptions. The risky bonds they had bought could not be sold – after all, if you buy something no one else wants to buy, you're not going to be able to sell them for precisely the same reason – no one else wants to buy.

Franklin Templeton eventually had to shutter its funds, disallowing redemptions and saying just this: If you let us wind this down over a long period of time, we believe you'll get back your money. Just don't ask for it right now.

This set off a chain of events where SEBI started investigating what exactly happened. And, of course, the investigation opened a new can of worms. The questions were: Why was Franklin Templeton (FT) the only AMC to shutter funds in this manner? Why didn't they follow due procedure for winding up a fund? Those answers may remain unclear but here's what we know.

First, we learnt that the former head of FT's APAC operations, Vivek Kudva, his wife, Roopa, and mother, Vasanthi, had sold all their holdings in those six schemes just before the schemes were shut down. Kudva appears to have had information about trouble; information that wasn't available publicly. Essentially, the funds had started to borrow to pay for redemptions, because their holdings were illiquid. Those borrowings had reached an extreme, at the time when Vivek Kudva and his family withdrew Rs 30 crore they had invested in these funds.

There were more charges detailed in the SEBI order of June 2021. FT had not adhered to the mandate of the six schemes; it had bought bonds rated as much more risky than the classification of these schemes allowed; it had bought long-term bonds and fudged the time frame to treat them as though they were shorter duration; it had refused to exit non-performing assets on multiple occasions when it had a chance to cut its losses.

The regulator took pretty drastic action. It asked FT to return about Rs 450 crore along with penal interest of 12 per cent to investors in those schemes – that amounts to over Rs 500 crore. It fined the Kudvas Rs 7 crore personally. It barred FT from offering any debt schemes for two years. And it tightened the classifications for debt funds and narrowed the mandates in the new classifications.

There may be appeals against the order and it's possible that the monetary punishments will be reduced. But the tighter classification stays for sure, and this will change the debt fund market.

The lesson here is that when Franklin gave those amazing returns, we might have assumed it was due to some magical intuition on the part of the fund manager. However, the magic just lay in taking a lot more risk than one would have expected of a debt fund.

Higher rewards usually involve higher risk, and if you think about it some more:

- The highest reward in the first half of 2021 was in bitcoin. And this fell 50 per cent in less than a week, in May 2021 alone. The risk is that the price can wipe out your capital before you know it. (Volatility.)
- Equity, over long periods of time, has given superlative returns. But there have been 30 per cent losses in the short term as well, if you watched in the interim.
- The lowest risk seems to be in short-term government securities. The government won't default. But the reward is just as low. (Russia and Argentina have also defaulted on government bonds so even these are not totally safe. Nothing is.)

What should make you suspicious is the offer of a high return at a 'low risk'. That just does not happen; go in with your eyes open, if you must.

And then you have international funds which give you exposure to markets outside India. Buy a Nasdaq 100 index fund. India currently doesn't have a great set of funds that target other countries, but Indian investors can invest rupees in a Hang Seng Index ETF (covering Hong Kong), a China fund by Edelweiss and a set of funds that combine global investing with Indian stocks, from houses like DSP and Parag Parikh.

The Direct, the Regular, the Growth, the Dividend: Confusion reigns

There are over 1700 schemes in mutual funds. Each one will also have dividend and growth options. And each of those subcategories also have regular and direct options. That's more than 6000 combinations.

This is insane. Mutual funds are supposed to help you invest in something because you don't understand how to invest. If you now need help to invest in mutual funds, isn't that missing the point entirely?

But fear not, because I'll tell you what these options are, and I'll tell you how they came about. You'll still be confused at the end, but the idea is to make you sound intelligent at parties.

First, a little look at how the economics of a mutual fund work.

Distribution: The only thing funds care about

Raj is a smart mutual fund manager. He knows his stocks, meets his companies regularly, and attends conference calls. He's good enough to generate awesome returns, if you give him money. But how can you even know he's good? The answer has always been: Someone needs to tell you.

Meaning, you need a human being called a 'distributor' to come to you and say this:
- There are lots of stocks, you don't have time to look at them
- So choose a mutual fund instead
- But there are so many mutual funds
- So I will help you find the good mutual fund managers among them
- See, look at Raj

Now no one does such things out of the goodness of their heart. You have to pay people to do this, so Raj will pay a 'commission' to Anjana, who distributes his mutual fund.

This is how the mutual funds scaled to reach a lot more people than the Rajs of the world could hope to reach on their own. After all, it was a non-tech world, where people couldn't get information easily.

Mutual funds then became dependent on the distribution system. After a year, things would go like this:

- Rocky, a new mutual fund manager, finds Anjana, the distributor and tells her, Listen Anjana, I'll give you a higher commission. Sell my fund instead.
- Anjana would think carefully and indeed Rocky is a decent fund manager, and there's nothing wrong in recommending his fund.
- But what about Raj? Nice guy indeed. But if the horse makes friends with the grass, what is he going to eat?
- So Anjana scouts for customers. Hey, there's you – and you've finished a year of investing in Raj's funds.
- 'Sir, I think we should exit the funds with Raj and move to Rocky's fund.'

This is not usually bad because perhaps Raj is going through a messy divorce and his performance has not been on par. But Raj also knows in his heart that it wasn't performance – it was the higher commission.

The complexity of the mutual fund industry is linked to the incentives that mutual fund distributors receive. And these can take many forms.

The entry load rigmarole

Mutual funds pay commissions to those that distribute them. This takes many forms. But first, the one you directly paid.

You pay as an **entry load**. That means when you buy a fund for Rs 1,00,000, you see only Rs 97,750 invested. Why? They deduct a 2.25 per cent 'entry load'. This was the case all the way till 2009.

Who gets the 2.25 per cent? Your distributor. You either went through a bank, or you went through a friendly neighbourhood uncle (or auntie) who sold you these funds. You don't pay them directly; the mutual fund does, through this entry load.

So this 'distributor' would call you every year and say, well, just move your money from one fund to another. They would then earn another 2.25 per cent from you. If you made 12 per cent, you might think this was okay, but consider this: An extra 2.25 per cent every year will take a Rs 1,00,000 investment to Rs 6,00,000 or so in 20 years.

Paying it one year and then staying put, for the same investment, would have taken it to Rs 9,40,000 in the same time.

Entry loads were banned in mutual funds in 2009, because of this massive abuse. Everyone complained but they quickly fell in line.

Commissions continued – now it was 'trail'

If you couldn't pay an entry load, how could you compensate a middleman? The answer was: High management fees.

Mutual funds are allowed to charge a fee to manage your money. Some of this fee goes for actual management charges, such as the salary of the fund manager, the cost of postage to send statements, the cost of maintaining the websites, etc.

But a very large part of it goes to the distributors who help you invest in funds. Such as banks and friendly relationship managers.

So when you invest Rs 1,00,000 in a fund, it may charge 2 per cent as management fee. So if the market goes up 12 per cent, they automatically take out 2 per cent and you get 10 per cent, ending up with just Rs 1,10,000.

So far so good, but what if you lose 10 per cent? They still take their 2 per cent, so you end up down 12 per cent, at Rs 88,000.

This sounds a little unfair – how can they charge you when they haven't made any money for you? Let me ask you this too – if your employer makes no money in a month, can they refuse to pay your salary? That would be unfair to you. So think of yourself as 'employing' the mutual fund to manage your money. That's what they are doing anyhow – just managing it. The losses are yours, and the gains are yours – they only keep their fees.

Out of this fee, the fund management company will pay their distributors. Since this fee is charged every year, the commissions can be paid every year. This is called a 'trail' investment.

To attract distributors, companies also paid 'upfront' commissions. Get us a customer and we'll pay you 1 per cent, they would say. And then if that customer stays till the end of the year, we'll pay you another 0.5 per cent.

A distributor is supposed to help you with your investments, but often they would simply do very little more than look at your face and ask you to sign somewhere. Bank relationship managers kept changing, so while you paid those commissions (through the fund management fees every year) you weren't exactly getting any service.

Further, as SEBI made mutual funds more open and transparent, anyone could easily see fund performances, portfolios and history, and compare these. You could now do this on your mobile phone while hanging from a metro strap. As more and more people got smart enough to choose their own funds, do their own investments and, in fact, manage everything for themselves, the question became: Why am I paying commissions to someone when I'm doing all the work?

The way it worked was: If you used a distributor 'code' in your purchase, the distributor would get commissions (for life) on your investment. If you didn't, well, the fund managers would still charge a high fee and pay the distributors a large sum of money (since you didn't have a distributor to pay).

Add to this the corporate ecosystem, where funds of corporate houses would be parked in short-term mutual funds. Corporates usually have their own treasury divisions that do all the analysis and transactions. So why were corporates paying commissions? There wasn't a choice.

Enter the direct fund

SEBI saw this and in 2013, the regulator decreed that every fund must also offer schemes in a no-commission mode. They called them 'direct' plans. No commissions would be made from such a plan, so the 'expense ratio' would be lower.

All current commissions paying plans would be called 'Regular' plans.

Meaning: You'd now have an ABC Equity Fund (Direct) that would charge a lower expense ratio, and an ABC Equity Fund (Regular) that would charge a higher one.

This sounds great. Except now you have to remember which one, and remember, there are 1000+ schemes, and each one gets two avatars.

Funnily enough, the portfolio of the two schemes was exactly the same. So you have the same fund manager, the same underlying stocks (or bonds) and different NAVs for direct and regular portions.

For the curious: There's no way to convert between the two – you have to sell one, and buy the other. This is considered a taxable sale, by the way!

Of course, the best way to do things is to go direct, for most of you reading this book. Why?

Aside: Why direct plans are better – Not just commissions

Think about it. If a 'direct' fund charges 1 per cent, but a 'regular' fund charges 1.5 per cent, you would expect that the performance would only be different by that much – 0.5 per cent. Meaning, if I gave Rs 1,00,000 to the same fund in direct and regular options, then the direct option might go up to Rs 1,10,000 (10 per cent up) while the regular should be up to Rs 1,09,500 (9.5 per cent). This is the mathematics.

But this maths is not the reality. In reality, you might find the regular fund is only up to Rs 1,08,700 (8.7 per cent). Why this difference? Let's just say there are things deeper in here that we don't understand. But the reality is that regular funds underperform by a lot more than just commission-based differences.

Having said that, why would anyone go for the regular fund at all?

Everyone who does work for you deserves to be paid. An adviser, and even a distributor that hand-holds you through an investment should get paid. If you must, pay them directly. Investing Rs 5,00,000? Pay, say, 1 per cent of that.

The thing is that people don't like to pay the adviser directly. So they end up getting sold the 'regular' funds instead. This way you don't pay from your pocket to the adviser. You pay in a complex, hidden way, and you actually pay a lot more! Even worse: You pay for life (as long as you're invested).

Paying forever is a mess. Your bank manager who sold you the mutual fund may no longer be around. And you'll still pay the bank a fee as long as you own the fund.

I'll just say avoid this and simply use the 'direct' option.

'Mind it,' as Rajinikanth would say! If you buy from a site that has 'direct' in its name, this usually means you will get the 'regular' plan. There are websites where you can buy the direct plan, but I'm afraid that by the time this book is published, these sites may not exist. I would choose to buy directly from the website of the mutual fund itself because the fund has to offer this or else, it gets a stern talking-to from SEBI.

Dividends and growth

You could buy a fund that pays out money regularly. After all, mutual funds also get money from their investments – the stocks they buy pay dividends. The bonds they buy pay interest. This 'income' can be passed on to you, or reinvested back into the fund.

You can choose to get this income as a dividend, by choosing the 'dividend' plan. This means the fund must pay out dividends regularly, and you get the income. This income is taxed (as of 2021).

If you choose the 'growth' option, you don't get any income, and the fund will use that income and reinvest it right back. This is great – you don't pay any taxes, and your money compounds itself.

Why would anyone choose 'dividends'? Again, this is history playing mean tricks. Earlier, dividends were not taxed at all, but selling a mutual fund was. So you wanted dividends even if it meant taking them out and reinvesting them back into the same fund. There were even 'automatic dividend reinvestment' options that did this for you. This gave rise to even 'daily dividend' options in mutual funds – when you could get a dividend every single day, and reinvest that back. To save tax. At which point, barbers lost serious revenue, because everyone in the mutual fund accounting industry tore their hair off.

The growth option is simpler. All the money stays in the fund, which reinvests any money it receives. If you want some money, you sell a few units, and that money is a 'capital gain', and gets taxed at a lower rate than dividend income (if you've held the fund for over a certain time period).

Selling a growth option fund regularly has another advantage. After three years from purchase (one year for equity funds) you get an even lower tax rate called the long-term capital gains tax rate. This is, as of 2021, 10 per cent for equity and 20 per cent for non-equity funds.

So the simple rule, even if you want 'income' from your funds, is:
- Buy the growth option
- Sell a little every month or quarter, and take home the income

Over time, this is a far more tax-efficient strategy.

Don't get suckered into advertising that makes you think, 'Oh, this fund pays dividend!' It's your own money that's being given back to you.

> *Note:* Mutual funds are tax-isolated. Unlike you, they don't pay any taxes when they get interest or dividends. This is another reason why investing through a fund makes sense.

Closed- versus open-ended

You would think a fund can be bought or sold any time you wanted. That's only in open-ended funds which are sold and redeemed directly by the fund house. But there are other cases where funds are 'closed-ended', where you can only buy in a New Fund Offer, and then at no other time. Even selling, or redemptions, are allowed by the AMC only after a period of time.

Why would anybody buy a closed fund? This allows people to lock their money in for a fixed period of time. Sometimes it can help save tax. The Indian tax laws allow you to adjust your purchase price up for inflation for long-term capital gains in debt funds. But a year is considered to be between April and March. If you buy a fund in March 2021, and it is sold in April 2024, the tax department thinks four years have passed, which gives you four years of inflation that is not taxed. For a return of 6 per cent where inflation is 4 per cent, the taxes you pay can drop substantially with closed-ended funds.

Closed-ended schemes are often sold aggressively. That's also because they provide high commissions. After all, if you're locked in for three years, then it's three years of fees that the AMC can see, so they share higher commissions to attract more distributors. As a buyer, you might end up losing all the tax benefits to higher commissions!

Suckered: A monthly dividend in an equity fund

'Dude, you're going to love this. BCBCB fund gives a monthly dividend!'

'Really? Do you know how it works?'

'No, don't tell me it's another scam. Wait, tell me. What is it?'

'Simple. They invest your money. Every month, they sell a few of their investments to pay you. It's your money that they give back to you and call it a monthly dividend.'

'So what's bad about it?'

'They're charging you a higher fee so that they can give you back your own money. You could just invest in one of their other funds that doesn't claim to play the monthly dividend god.'

'I shouldn't bother about a monthly dividend then?'

'If you get it, you're going to pay a high tax on it. If you really want the monthly income, just set up a systematic withdrawal plan in one of their simpler funds.'

'Why don't they tell me this?'

'Well, how else are they going to sell you something new and shiny, my friend? It's the circle of life. Just don't be the one that's dying.'

Oh, there's also risk in debt funds

Debt funds are thought of as safe vehicles but the devil lies in the details. We've described the FT debacle, for example. Given that mutual funds publish their portfolios every month, you can quickly see what lies within the portfolios of each of the funds you own. The red flags are:

(a) **Perpetual bonds with a 'call' date:** There are banking bonds and other perpetual bonds where the concept is: We'll take your money and never pay you back the principal (hence, perpetual). We'll pay higher interest rates (if we pay at all). Also on some day in the future we have the right (but not the obligation) to pay you back the principal and cancel the bonds. Mutual funds buy such bonds in the hope that they will give great returns, and still be bought back (which returns the principal). After the fiascos of Yes Bank and DHFL, where the company could not pay back the money (either principal or interest), these mutual funds had to take a hit. More meaningfully, you, as an investor in such funds, would have taken a hit. Perpetual bonds can be dangerous.

(b) **Last year's returns don't matter:** People buy funds after they have done well in a given year. But debt funds are slaves to interest rate cycles. If rates fall, they make money. If rates go up, they lose money.

Here's why rate cuts are profitable for debt funds. Say, there's Rs 100 in fixed deposit at 8 per cent interest, maturing a year later to yield Rs 108. The next day, the Reserve bank of India (RBI) cuts interest rates so much that new FDs are now offering 6 per cent. If you could sell the FD, then someone should be willing to pay Rs 101.90 for it, to get the same 6 per cent since if you invest 101.90 and get back 108 in a year, your return is 6 per cent. This is why, when rates go down, the price of a bond (which is like a tradeable FD) goes up. Debt funds hold portfolios of bonds, which gain value when rates fall, and lose money when rates go up.

After a cycle has plateaued, you can expect interest rates to reverse direction, or maybe remain stable. The debt funds cannot make the same profits they did in the past. Disappointments then cause people to exit, possibly at the wrong time, because the cycle may change again.

(c) **Companies on the verge of disaster borrow and default:** Reliance Communications was backed by one of India's richest families, but it still went bankrupt. When the trouble becomes known, a mutual fund manager may no longer be able to sell securities issued by that company. So they remain in the fund's portfolio and this can hurt you as an investor if they default.

You must assume the mutual fund architecture requires all risk be taken by you, the investor. The debt fund, which is considered safe, might be so 99 per cent of the time. But live long enough, and chase enough in the way of high-return debt, and you'll experience the other 1 per cent, which they don't tell you about.

The debt fund classification matrix

With the Franklin saga, SEBI has changed how debt funds need to reveal their risk in two directions, to the public.

- **Interest rate risk:** If there's a change in interest rates, how heavily is the fund impacted? The answer to that lies in how much time is remaining on the bonds they hold, in terms of time to maturity. A more mathematical term is 'duration', which tells us how much impact the bonds will see in the price if the interest rate were to change. SEBI divides this into short term (duration of less than one year), medium (up to three years) and long term (more than three).
- **Credit risk:** This is effectively the risk of your not getting your money back. The risk is on the unitholders. So they classify 'low' credit risk as only the most pristine of securities. (Government bonds and very highly rated PSUs and corporates will qualify.) Medium credit risk is just a couple notches lower in terms of rating. Everything else is 'high' credit risk.

Type of risk	Low credit risk	Medium credit risk	High credit risk
Short duration	Super safe funds (many liquid funds)	Some short-term funds that go into slightly lower rated corporates	A short-term fund that's taking very high risk (e.g. Franklin)
Medium duration	Typically, shorter-term gilt, banking or PSU bond funds	Many corporate bond funds, medium-duration funds and dynamic bond funds	Most credit risk funds
Long duration	Gilt funds, mostly. But some PSU and banking funds will also be here	Some corporate bond funds, dynamic bond funds, long-term bond funds	Very unlikely to see anyone here. Should only be credit risk funds

A fund can only choose to be in one of these boxes. If the portfolio they hold changes over time, and they land up with higher risk, they are required to inform unitholders.

What you should do is select only the low- and medium-risk boxes in either interest rate or credit risk, especially when you don't understand the debt market. (If you did, you wouldn't need advice!)

So do you now get it?

There's a choice for regular and there's direct. In each, you choose from growth or dividend:
- There are forty fund houses to add to the mix
- With mutual funds the fun will never end

All those choices sound extreme, but they create jobs. People who know them can sound intelligent enough to sell you something. The funds can ensure the menu cards remain full. People like me get to write books on 'why'. More options, more GDP.

The whole purpose of places like Starbucks is for people with no decision-making ability whatsoever to make six decisions just to buy one cup of coffee. Short, tall, light, dark, caf, decaf, low-fat, non-fat, etc. So people who don't know what the hell they're doing or who on earth they are can, for only $2.95, get not just a cup of coffee but an absolutely defining sense of self: Tall. Decaf. Cappuccino. – Joe Fox, You've Got Mail

Managed accounts: The PMS and AIF choices

I've founded a company that runs a Portfolio Management Service (PMS). Here, the SEBI mandated minimum investment is Rs 50 lakh, and the manager gets to decide how to deploy your money, much like a mutual fund, but with two specific differences:
- The investments are made in your name, so you retain the ownership and voting rights. In a mutual fund, it's the fund that owns the stock and will vote – you have no say.
- The portfolio manager can also take a portion of profits as his fees, apart from an annual management fee. Mutual funds cannot share in the profits of your investments.

Given that an investment like this would be a minimum of Rs 50 lakh, they tend to be for the well-heeled. Since managers are allowed to take a share of the profits, where the fund manager will say, 'I understand how the system works, so I'll take greater risk for greater awards', these tend to be the daring, risk-taking variety of investments.

Not all portfolio managers are like that, of course. The idea of such a service is not only to take high risks, even if the minimum seems to imply that, by virtue of a belief that if you're rich enough to give Rs 50 lakh to someone, you can afford higher risks.

In reality, what more well-heeled people want is the ability to diversify into multiple types of asset classes. Some will demand simplicity in terms of an investment process. Others ask for an allocation to India+USA with the ability to outsource the discipline of balancing the two. Not all portfolio managers demand a share of profits (we don't, for instance) and not many charge exorbitant fees.

Such services, however, may not have the transparency provided by mutual funds in terms of returns, what they hold, and how often they churn. This information must be obtained privately from each PMS separately. It is suitable for those that have the ability to understand their investments better so that they can take the kind of risk they're comfortable with, while a manager does the heavy lifting. Or, in the case of an asset allocation-style PMS, the investor wants to outsource the act of deploying money into a combination of safe and risky investments according to their own risk profile.

There's also the concept of an alternative investment fund (AIF). Such investments allow people to invest in early- or late-stage private companies (venture capital) or in fixed income instruments from corporates. There's another variety that allows people to invest in stocks or derivatives, with a little twist: Leverage.

In certain cases, markets allow you to invest one rupee and benefit as if you had invested two. If the investment doubles, you make four times your money. In the same vein, if the investment falls by half, you lose all your money. It's a double-edged sword, but double-edged swords are often the weapon of choice for people who know, or think they know, how to handle them. The AIF affords you a leverage of two times your investment, with the assumption that the manager is adept enough to not let you lose all your money.

Such AIFs require you to invest at least Rs 1 crore which means it's for the relatively rich among us. Using leverage requires a more discerning and knowledgeable investor, who is also wealthy enough to afford to punt on such a product.

The concept of PMS and AIF is for someone who needs special attention compared to a mutual fund investor. Often, people already have mutual funds and dabble in a PMS in addition. Many use PMS (like ours) for asset allocation and discipline. In general, avoid over aggression and promises of returns that will take you to the moon – whether in mutual funds, or in PMS/AIF.

A sample fund choice

One way to meaningfully select your mutual funds is to first map your requirements. You may have different needs: You need to plan for your children's education, your own retirement, a down payment for a house, etc.

Each of these goals will have a different time frame and a different rupee number to target. Consider just one goal: Retirement.

1. Work on asset allocation: How much debt (low risk) and how much equity (high risk) should you own? The answer to this

question lies almost entirely in how much time you have left before retirement (or to any goal).
   a. More than ten years left: You can go more than 80 per cent equity.
   b. Three to ten years left: You can go between 50 per cent and 80 per cent equity.
   c. Less than three years: You can go for 30 per cent equity or so.
   d. If you don't want to know, just use 50 per cent equity, 50 per cent debt.
2. Second, work on the equity allocation.
   a. If you don't have time, choose index funds for equity:
      i. 33 per cent India top 50
      ii. 33 per cent India second rung
      iii. 33 per cent US top 100
3. Fixed income fund choices – a banking and PSU debt fund and a gilt fund work reasonably well.
4. Always go for direct plans, and the growth option. All other options are sub-optimal.
5. Track your status every six months, and you might choose to invest in an SIP mode (monthly investment) to even out any timing issues.

Does this always work? No. But in general, this combination will suit a lot of people over the long term (more than five years).

What do these terms mean?

Definitions of commonly used terms that sound nice, but often hide what they really mean.

AMC: The asset management company. Or, the company that takes the fees from the mutual funds you invest in, and actually invests and manages the money.

AUM: This is not a Buddhist chant. It is short for 'Assets Under Management'. This is often a fund manager chant. AUM is essentially all the money the mutual fund scheme is managing. Why don't they just call them 'assets', we will never know. But AUM is what it's all about.

Expense ratio: How much does the mutual fund pay the AMC? The answer is the expense ratio, or the TER (the 'total' expense ratio). Total, because you have different kinds of expenses – the management fee, the custodian fee, the SEBI fee, the education fee, and the fee to buy face masks for the guards who stop you from throwing things at the AMC for charging too many types of fees.

NAV: The net asset value of the fund. You buy 'units' of a fund. If a fund has 100 units and the stocks it owns are worth Rs 500, your NAV is Rs 5 per unit. If I come in with Rs 250 and buy 50 more units at this Rs 5, there's 150 units, but the fund's AUM is now Rs 750. Imagine this grows to Rs 1200 because some company it has a stake in found lithium (oil is passé). So the NAV goes up to Rs 8 per unit.

Why is it 'net'? Well, there may be some liabilities – money the fund is supposed to pay. For example, it's bought some stocks today, but the money's due tomorrow, and the stocks will be transferred the day after that. The fund may have borrowed money temporarily. Net all those out, and you have net assets. Divide net assets by units and you have NAV.

SIP: A systematic investment plan. The idea is that if you invest regularly in something, it'll grow to make you a lot of money. A SIP makes a lot of sense, unless you already have a lot of money to invest, maybe because you've received an inheritance, or a bonus or you've cashed in stock options at the start-up where you work. At which point they'll tell you to do a lump sum instead.

Lump sum: This is when you put in a single investment rather than promise to do a regular SIP. You could do it with a lot of money, or with very little. An SIP is, in fact, a set of lump sums invested over time.

SWP: The systematic withdrawal plan. Invest once, and take out money regularly. This is for the kind of people that have got a salary forever. So when they retire, they feel lost without an SMS that tells them fresh money has come into the bank account. So they use an SWP. It's not a bad thing, but it's like taking out money regularly to feed a behavioural void. The real answer might be to take money only when you need it, and let the money grow when you don't. But there's too many edge cases here for one to give definitive advice. The old folks that don't understand technology, for example. The people who, if they had a lump sum, would instantly find a way to spend it, so the SWP protects them from themselves. Like I said, the behavioural void. Do it if you feel you must.

STP: The systematic transfer plan. This is where you invest in one thing but withdraw from it to systematically invest (transfer) in another thing. Say, you receive a lump sum as above. You don't want to put it into equity funds. So you buy a liquid fund and do an STP into an equity fund instead. This eases you into the equity market, slowly, over time. You can just keep filling cash into the liquid fund whenever you get extra money.

CAGR: The compound annual growth rate (CAGR) is simply a mechanism to understand how one particular investment has performed. If you invest Rs 1000 and it becomes Rs 2000 in five years, then the CAGR is about 14 per cent.

The formula is: Amount = Principal × (1+CAGR)^Period

XIRR: A complex term that's an extended internal rate of return. Think of it like this. I invested Rs 1000 five years ago and it became Rs 2000. What's my return? Simple – run a formula and it's roughly 14 per cent per annum (CAGR).

But what if I did a monthly investment of Rs 20 for five years, and it became Rs 2000? You might think – hey, I invested Rs 1200 (sixty months, Rs 20 a month) but I only got Rs 2000, so shouldn't it be around 10.7 per cent, if you use the return calculator?

No. Your return is a whopping 20 per cent. This is because the sum is invested over time, rather than all at once. The Rs 20 you invested sixty months ago has earned interest for that whole period while the Rs 20 you invested last month has earned interest for only one month.

Most of us don't invest all our money at one time, or even monthly. We may skip a few months. We may add more because we have a bonus. We may even withdraw at certain times. The XIRR tells you what kind of returns you have made on your spread-out investments, assuming that all your investments had the exact same return.

In mathematical terms it's a weighted combination of the CAGR of each investment.

WALKING THE TALK

A practical approach to investing

How should you invest?

So exactly what should you invest in? We've talked about the complexities, the nuances and the things you should fear. What should you do?

Here's a summary. But first, understand this:
- I don't know your personal situation. Nothing in finance is 'generalized'
- So what we'll do is prepare a template. You figure out what applies to you, and act accordingly.

The hygiene

You need to handle emergency funds and insurance first. Get those right. Here's a quick summary (see flowchart on page 82).

Always get the emergency funding right and do it first. If you hate your job, or your boss is harassing you, you're going to need this just to be able to move on without anxiety. This is also crucial if your company shuts down, or you have to stop working for some other reason.

On Life Insurance, the question you must really answer is: *If I die today, how much will my dependants need to live the rest*

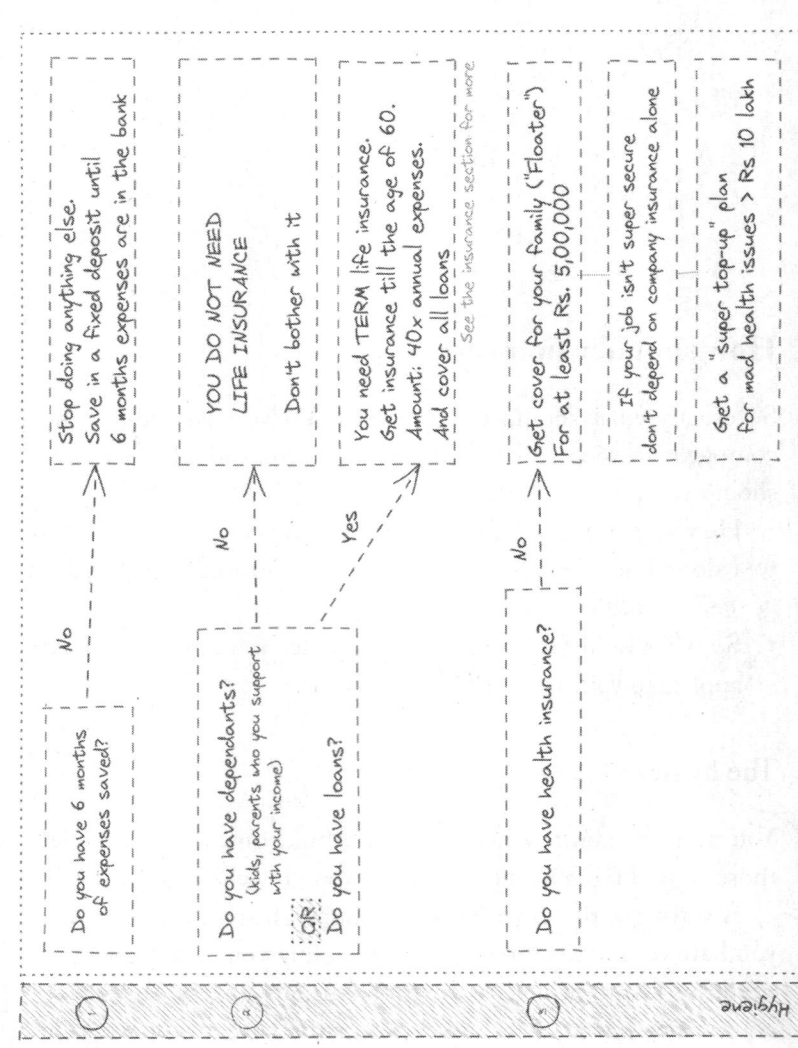

of their lives? The answer is different for different people, but take a rough calculation of 40 years of expenses and account for inflation.

We've spoken about health before, so we'll keep it simple.

The strategy

Before you jump into actual investments, here's a way to plan how to divide your savings, either on a monthly basis, or as a lump sum, into risk capital (stocks) and low risk (fixed income)

We aren't including real estate or gold in these calculations. Those are different beasts. I wouldn't recommend either purely as an investment. You buy a house to live in, sure. Beyond that, dabbling in real estate is like running a speculative business. We'll come to gold separately.

Now how do you divide your money? Plan your long-term goals.

- First, if you don't know what to do, just put 50 per cent of your money in the risk bucket, and 50 per cent in non-risk. This is simple enough.
- If you want more granularity, let's get to the questions you need to answer.

Your children's college education

You're likely to be able to take care of your children's schooling entirely from your monthly income. That's a good thing. However, you will get this big 'hit' when the time comes, to pay for your children's college education. This can be saved in stages.

You can make a quick estimate on how much you're going to need for their college expenses. If your child is eight years old,

Do you have children?

School expenses: Pay from your salary

College:
When they turn 18

Rough plan:
Today's expenses: 40L
In 10 years: 80L
Inflation: 5%

Allocate

Turn 18:	Equity	Fixed Income
10+ years away	100%	0%
5-10 years	70%	30%
1-5 years	30%	70%
Less than a year	0%	100%

How much do you need to retire?

Point at which you don't work because you need the money — you work because you want to

Rough calculation:

Annual expenses * Years to retire * 3

A (31) year old spending Rs 1,00,000 a month

Needs (after 29 years)

1,00,000 * 12 * 29 * 3 = 10.44 cr.

How?**

Age	Save % of income	Equity	Fixed income
30-40	30%	100%	0%
40-45	40%	70%	30%
45+**	40%	50%	50%

** Assuming some savings exist
* Illustration only. Risk taking ability differs by individual circumstance.

Add it all up: How much needs to go to equity each month, and fixed income

---

Do you have loans?

Insurance should cover loans

Credit card debt? PAY IT BACK FIRST.

Pay off loans: Highest interest rate first.

Loan EMI be less than 25% of income

then fees for college will be needed ten years later, when she's eighteen. If you think a college education costs Rs 40 lakh today, you'll need around Rs 80 lakh then.

This is not as difficult to achieve as you may think. Starting from zero, you can invest Rs 35,000 a month, and at 10 per cent returns, you'll get there in ten years. (This assumes you can scale up the savings by 5 per cent extra every year.)

But you needn't start from zero. You can allocate part of your current savings to this long-term goal, and put that in a specific bucket which you handle separately from your other savings. The amount depends on how many kids you have, and how many years there are to go before they start college.

Once you've taken care of emergencies, insurance, and long-term goals like kids' education, you allocate what's left to risk and non-risk. This exercise gives you a number – both of the savings you can allocate now, and of the amount you need to have per month additionally.

Keep this in mind. Let's now look at:

Your own retirement

If you spend Rs 1,00,000 per month today and you're thirty-one years old, you are likely to spend Rs 4,00,000 per month or so by the time you're sixty (at 5 per cent inflation). To generate that much, and then more, for the rest of your life, assuming you live till the ripe old age of ninety, you'll need Rs 10.44 crore at the time you retire.

A simple formula for you is:

Amount you need = Annual Expenses Now × Years remaining to retirement × 3

Note: Only apply this formula if you have at least ten years left to retirement. If you're closer to retirement the standard formula doesn't work; you will need more money. Here's a table that will help.

Expenses per month			Rs 1,00,000
Inflation	5%	Retire at (age)	60
Return	7%	Plan till (age)	90

Age	Expenses at retirement (Rs)	Corpus needed (Rs)	Rough calculation (Rs)
30	4,32,194	11,20,86,694	10,80,00,000
35	3,38,635	8,78,22,858	9,00,00,000
40	2,65,330	6,88,11,507	7,20,00,000
45	2,07,893	5,39,15,616	5,40,00,000
50	1,62,889	4,22,44,296	3,60,00,000
55	1,27,628	3,30,99,511	1,80,00,000
59	1,05,000	2,72,31,050	36,00,000

This also can be achieved reasonably easily. Put about 30 per cent of your post-tax income into savings, and if it grows at 10 per cent, you should see yourself reach the Rs 11 crore mark by the time you retire.

And then, as you grow older, you want to reduce your risk. In your thirties, you can take higher risks, so even 100 per cent equity allocation is okay. In your forties and fifties, you may need to reduce the risk you take. Taper down to 20 per cent equity by retirement.

Note: If you have loans, or high debt, you can't take that much risk, so adjust your estimates accordingly.

Applying this framework as an example:

	Time left (years)	Start with	Invest monthly	Equity per cent	Fixed income per cent	Starting Equity	Starting Fixed income	Ongoing Equity	Ongoing Fixed income
Child's education	10	5,00,000	30,000	70%	30%	3,50,000	1,50,000	21,000	9,000
Retirement	20	10,00,000	40,000	50%	50%	5,00,000	5,00,000	20,000	20,000
Total						8,50,000	6,50,000	41,000	29,000

This gives us an idea now of the strategy for the days ahead. Now for the tactics.

The Tactics

At this point you are going to have to make some tough decisions for yourself. Do you have the **time** to take all the investing decisions yourself?

Or the **inclination**: Is this really your cup of tea? Do you want to go down the rabbit hole of numbers and find that one little exciting thing that swings your long-term decisions?

Or **the ability or skill**? Not everyone's good at this kind of thing. You will, at some point, be road kill, when the market runs all over you. You're going to have to decide whether being an 'active' investor is for you.

Don't get me wrong. It's isn't like I'm saying you'll even know the answers. Some people do. Some people think they do, but soon realize they had the wrong answer. Others discover a passion for money deep inside themselves and go on to become good investors. The point is, be who you are, and don't try to change your entire life for this. There are alternative paths to prosperity.

The **passive route** is for those who don't have the time or inclination or skill. Here you know what has to go into equity and what is in debt (from the strategy discussion).

Then, you can just use a combination of Indian index funds – a large-cap index fund, a mid-cap index fund and an international index fund. At the time of writing, we'd suggest a Nifty Index fund, a Next-50 Index funds (ICICI has both) and then, a US Nasdaq 100 Fund (Motilal or Kotak).

On the fixed income side, you choose a simpler mechanism.

Do you have the
- ☐ Time
- ☐ Inclination
- ☐ Ability

To actively manage your investments?

No way! → **The Passive Route**

Yes, bring it on! → **The Active Route**

The Passive Route

Equity
- ☐ Nifty Index Fund
- ☐ Mid-cap Index Fund
- ☐ International Index Fund

in equal proportions

Fixed income
- ☐ Gilt Fund
- ☐ PSU and Banking Fund

in equal proportions

The Active Route

Equity

Mutual Funds:
Find active outperforming funds
Invest regularly

Stocks:
Select approach (trend, momentum, fundamental)
Select stocks
Invest in them regularly
Rebalance every year

Fixed income

Mutual Funds:
Find active outperforming funds
Invest regularly

Bonds:
Select approach (trend, momentum, fundamental)
Find bonds or derivatives
Invest regularly
Track and rebalance for concentration risks, etc.

Tactics

Government securities for the long term, since they aren't likely to default and have some safety, and PSU and banking debt funds for the short term. These may provide a slightly higher return sometimes, but there's less fear of default, given the bank and/or PSU tag.

This does it. Just split the money equally, and don't bother too much about markets going up, or down. All you care about is your asset allocation – are you wildly deviating from your chosen risk? Dial the risk down by selling some equity funds and buying fixed income funds, or dial it up by moving some cash from fixed income funds to equity.

The **active route** is where things get subjective. I hope this book would have helped open your mind to the range of possibilities and taught you a few things.

For actively selecting mutual funds, you need to regularly assess performance – perhaps once a year, or once in six months. Then a careful selection of top funds in each kind of strategy makes sense. Some mid-cap, some small-cap and some large-cap, with perhaps a tactically temporary addition of certain sector funds when a sector looks poised to change direction. Add in international and gold funds and you have a lot of choices.

Selecting funds is difficult because the information changes often, and you have to read the literature carefully. Understanding the fund manager's thought processes is also useful for fund selection.

This applies for fixed income mutual funds as well. Select a combination of funds that may have different durations (ultra-short term, low duration, long term) or add different types of funds (PSU and banking, corporate bond, credit risk or dynamic) to the mix. This is of course a skill by itself, but the learning process is key to understanding the specifics of each kind of fund.

After selection, you have to just continue to invest regularly. You could of course also go the **direct stocks route**.

Aside: What about gold?

Gold is loved by Indian investors. We've always loved gold, and it has been a source of decent inflation-adjusted returns in the past. However, the shiny metal intrinsically does very little other than look good in decorative jewellery.

If you buy physical gold in the form of jewellery, there are several problems:
- You have no idea of the quality of the gold you buy – you must trust a jeweller. This jeweller may not be around when you need to sell the gold, and the other person you go to can quickly say: Oh, this is fake gold, and I won't give you much for this.
- You pay extremely high 'making' charges. If you buy from a jeweller, and then sell back the very same day, they will buy it back from you at 5 per cent to 10 per cent discount. That is a very high cost. And then, you end up paying about 3 per cent GST (Goods and Services Tax) each way.
- Safety is a concern. Gold is dense, so you can store a 1 kg bar inside your belt buckle. It's easy to steal.
- Finally, it's not easy to sell physical gold. There are emotional consequences. People believe gold is the last thing to sell, so they don't sell it – in that context, it's a lousy emergency instrument because you need something you can sell easily and without regret, in an emergency.

But you can use different instruments, such as gold bonds, or gold mutual funds, which save you the trouble of handling physical gold or trusting jewellers (remember Nirav Modi is a jeweller!). The best might be a sovereign gold bond, issued by the government – this bond gives you interest and pays back the price of gold in seven years after issue.

The fundamental issue with gold is that it's actually an instrument of fear, a hedge against inflation, or a nasty government. Increasingly, though, as the world gets more financially aware, it makes more sense to bet governments will survive. Gold is one of India's largest imports and the government is trying hard to reduce this. Over time, if they are successful, the price of gold too will correct downwards.

Having said that, it's logical and better to invest in a productive asset instead. Stocks and bonds provide dividends or interest, and contribute to economic growth. Gold does very little in terms of being a productive asset, and as we start to realize that we might just lose our fascination for the shiny metal.

Fixing your portfolio

Typically, a lot of us have done strange things in the past and we have no idea where to begin to fix these. So

1. **Get a handle on things**: Find out where your money is, and put that down on a spreadsheet. Tabulate all the mutual funds, stocks and other investments you own.
2. **Build your strategy**: Get yourself a debt to equity ratio based on your goals, and thought processes, as described above.
3. **Decide on tactics**: Will you continue your current investments or move them to a more passive set? If you stay, should you

just get rid of the weakest investments? My view is that if anything is less than 1 per cent of your portfolio, it's not worth keeping – so you could use that as a starting point to re-evaluate your current portfolio.
4. **Plan a transition:** Once you know your debt–equity ratio, you might decide you hold way too many funds or investments. If that's the case, plan a transition into what you will do next. You may need to plan for taxation, transaction costs and timing.

This can be done over months or quarters, rather than all at once. There are many online resources to learn and grow.

Always remember this: If it's too complicated to understand, you shouldn't have it.

Should you get an adviser?

Yes, if life is complicated enough for you to do so.

For people with large portfolios, inheritance issues, succession planning and such, the services of a good investment adviser can be invaluable. At the same time, it's useful to know your options, so you must keep yourself informed about the options that are available.

Remember this: In the end, it's your money. Advisers come in all shapes and sizes, and you have to be aware that some may not have your best interests in mind. You can pay for good advice (you're doing that if you buy this book!). But be aware that sometimes, even the free advice you get turns out to be way too expensive.

Does age matter?

Yes and no.

Some people don't have the time to think about all this when they're managing kids, what with school and homework and all that. They should go passive.

Some will have time when they're younger, or older, and will want to learn. The active route is useful for them. You can of course shift between styles when you like. In fact, you could even have a passive and an active portfolio – the passive for the growth, and the active for, well, scratching that itch.

It might help to think of investing in terms of life cycle as you grow up, grow older and then retire.

In your twenties, your needs are different from later on in life. You need an emergency fund and perhaps another little fund for a sabbatical. You probably have fewer responsibilities; with luck, your parents are still hale and hearty, you don't have health problems (we hope), and you may not have a spouse or kids. You want to travel the world. Just go passive and use a 'goal' to save enough for your hobbies. You needn't plan for children's education just yet, but you do need a little to save for retirement. Oh, and no term life insurance either.

In your thirties, you're going to need to plan for children, if applicable. And perhaps, make a down payment for a house and adjust your lifestyle if you take an EMI mortgage. And plan for retirement, as usual. But you might want some part of your savings in active stocks, the other part in passive investments.

As you grow older, you're going to want more fixed income options to cover your liquidity needs just in case. Indian banks offer better fixed deposit returns for depositors above 60, and the government has special schemes (Pradhan Mantri Vaya

Vandana Yojana [PMVVY] and Senior Citizen Saving Scheme [SCSS] at the time this went to print). These can help you change your tactics.

Over time, you'll want to evolve the plan or plans that work best for you. The above process is just a framework that you can start with.

How do you plan for your children's education?

You have a child. You want the best for her. Or him. (Sometimes both. But, for now, let's use one gender.)

So you want to save for her future. When she is born you don't have any idea about what it will take. You're mostly clueless about parenthood, and you have probably figured out that the financials of diapers, doctors, vaccines, toys and nannies are the GDP of a large nation.

And therefore, you are going to be mis-sold bad products by bankers. Since you have no clue, you will buy that product named 'child protection plan'. Only slowly do you realize that while the 'child' is yours, the 'protection' is of their unnaturally high commissions.

So what to do?

Firstly, understand that unless you live in a fool's paradise, Rs 12 lakh is not going to be anywhere close to enough to meet your kids' education needs.

At about 5 per cent inflation and a cost of about Rs 18 lakh today, an undergraduate degree will cost you about Rs 40 lakh in 18 years.

For studies abroad, multiply a current cost (of, say, Rs 35 lakh) by 2.5 for a similar number.

Note: If your child is already older, then you adjust accordingly. How? Say your daughter is five years old. Then you want to calculate the college education fees when she's 18. That's how much? 18 lakh today = Rs 34 lakh in 13 years.

Wait, Rs 40 lakh is too much!

I can only save Rs 5000 per month, how will I even get to Rs 34 lakh or Rs 40 lakh?

The answer: It's not that bad.

Let's make two assumptions:
1. That your savings will go up by, say, 6 per cent a year. (Earnings increase due to inflation and thus, savings also go up.)
2. That, in the long term, you can get a return of 12 per cent a year from a stock market investment.

Then, if you start with Rs 5000 a month today, you will get to Rs 40 lakh in sixteen years. (In the sixteenth year from now, you'll be putting in Rs 12,000 a month.)

Saving for college: Rs 5000 a month at 12% per year return

Year	Invest	Start with	Return	End with
1	60,000	60,000	3,413	63,413
2	63,600	1,27,013	11,660	1,38,672
3	67,416	2,06,088	21,421	2,27,509
4	71,461	2,98,970	32,918	3,31,889
5	75,749	4,07,637	46,400	4,54,037
6	80,294	5,34,331	62,150	5,96,481
7	85,111	6,81,592	80,489	7,62,081
8	90,218	8,52,299	1,01,782	9,54,081
9	95,631	10,49,712	1,26,440	11,76,153
10	1,01,369	12,77,521	1,54,931	14,32,452

contd...

...contd

Year	Invest	Start with	Return	End with
11	1,07,451	15,39,903	1,87,782	17,27,685
12	1,13,898	18,41,583	2,25,592	20,67,175
13	1,20,732	21,87,907	2,69,036	24,56,943
14	1,27,976	25,84,919	3,18,881	29,03,799
15	1,35,654	30,39,453	3,75,990	34,15,443
16	1,43,793	35,59,237	4,41,342	40,00,579

And that's not an impossibly expensive way to plan for putting your daughter through college!

What about school?

School's more complex. You have to pay fees each year. You could just save that much every year. So if school costs you Rs 1,20,000 a year now, you will have to save Rs 10,000 a month now. And increase this amount by inflation every year.

You could optimize this somewhat. An algorithm to save for a few years (before your child begins school) will reduce the amount required. Let's say you get more safe for school and only get 10 per cent on your investment. Then you can put about Rs 8,200 every month, increasing by inflation (6 per cent) every year, and you'll be able to pay the increasing school fee too:

Saving for school: Rs 8200 a month at 10% per year return

Age	Invest	Fee	Return	End with
2	–	–	–	–
3	98,400	–	9,840	1,08,240
4	1,04,304	–	21,254	2,33,798
5	1,10,562	–	34,436	3,78,945
6	1,17,196	1,51,497	34,450	3,78,945

contd...

...contd

Age	Invest	Fee	Return	End with
7	1,24,228	1,60,587	34,259	3,76,844
8	1,31,681	1,70,222	33,830	3,72,134
9	1,39,582	1,80,436	33,128	3,64,408
10	1,47,957	1,91,262	32,110	3,53,214
11	1,56,835	2,02,737	30,731	3,38,042
12	1,66,245	2,14,902	28,939	3,18,324
13	1,76,219	2,27,796	26,675	2,93,422
14	1,86,793	2,41,464	23,875	2,62,627
15	1,98,000	2,55,951	20,468	2,25,143
16	2,09,880	2,71,308	16,371	1,80,086
17	2,22,473	2,87,587	11,497	1,26,469
18	2,35,821	3,04,842	5,745	63,193

Wait, what about marriage?

Look, if you educate them, they'll figure out their own marriage.

No, you still want to pay for their weddings? Okay, so here's what it will take, similar to college education calculations. A marriage might cost Rs 20 lakh today. If you think your daughter will marry when she's thirty, and she's two years old today, you are looking at a cost of Rs 1.28 crore.

Sounds extremely high? It costs just Rs 3000 a month (increased every year by 6 per cent) to get there. Again, we assume a return of 12 per cent on your money!

So, in total . . . we need:
- Rs 8200 a month for school
- Rs 5000 a month for college
- Rs 3000 a month for marriage

Which means, if your child is aged two, you would need about Rs 16,200 a month saved and parked for her. This is how it goes.

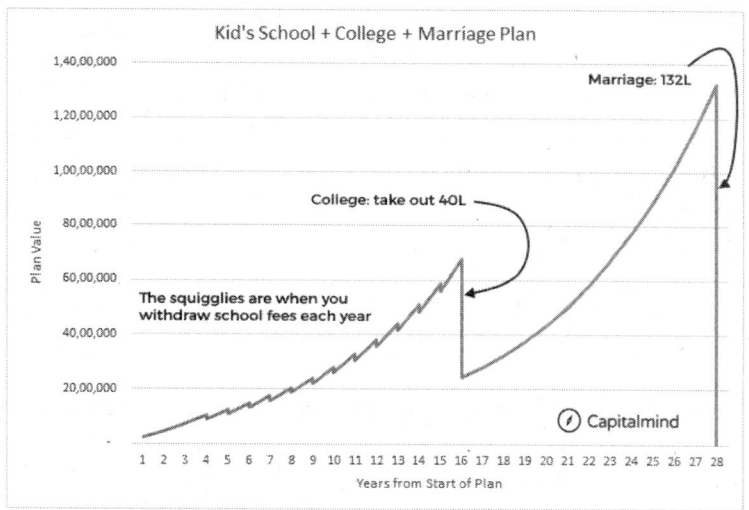

We do have caveats

You might get a higher (or lower) return. Every year will not be a constant return. So your actual 'curve' will be different, but it will roughly look like this in the long term.

Inflation assumptions will change over years. You'll have to change this graph to reflect that. Remember, if inflation falls, so will return expectations, and so will the required future costs.

The concept

Once you're clear that this is what you need to save to handle your child's education and other needs, you have an amount of money you invest per month.

The tactics are simple, and described in many ways earlier in this book. Your investment should be based on what kind of person you are and the risk you would like to take. Exactly what should you do to get the 12 per cent return you have assumed? The answer lies in a combination of debt and equity.

If you're conservative, choose only long-term government bonds yielding 6 per cent and be done with it. You'll just have to invest more money instead. To invest in something is a tactical choice.

The above calculation is enough to take you there, but you will need to course-correct if assumptions change.

The afterlife: Planning for what happens after you die

What Covid-19 has taught us is that life is brittle. You could be healthy, eat the right thing, do 100 push-ups a day, do your 10,000 steps religiously or whatever it takes to be in the best of health, and yet, a virus RNA with a little spike protein can knock the breath out of you. Literally.

In this context, we need to be aware that our life won't necessarily have a happy ending – it could end in an untimely death. This is a good enough reason to live life well when you can, simply because you are alive. But there's another thing to take care of: The people you will leave behind. When a loved one dies, remember that there is grief, but you must not leave your family to cope with a sense of utter helplessness.

What I speak of is the helplessness of not knowing how to take care of their financial life after you're gone. You're the one reading this book, so you obviously have some interest in the various aspects of managing money for your family. Often, we find there's only one such person in a small family that cares enough to track the finances. And when that one person passes on, the rest of the family struggles to piece things together.

Let's take this in two parts. First, we'll talk about what you should do to leave your family relatively secure. Second, you may be called upon to help a family, whose finance-in-charge has abruptly passed on, and what you can do to help.

For yourself there are some simple thumb rules. Let's look at them in order.

Get all your information together in one place. Bank accounts and numbers, demat and trading accounts, mutual fund accounts, and so on. Put all this information in a spreadsheet and ensure that at least one other person has access to this spreadsheet. Preferably two persons.

You might want to use a password manager to store your passwords, instead of keeping them open. (Ensure someone else has access to the password manager just in case.) Keep a list of all the following.

- Bank accounts – all of them including the numbers: You might be using fingerprint-based apps to download them, in which case just leave your phone access password with your significant other.
- Mutual fund information: Ensure that you retain information about which email ID is linked to the mutual funds you have invested in.
- Insurance policies: This should be obvious, but usually is not. Also put information on what insurance your credit cards may have.
- Loans: All your loan information, with details on how to access your logins.
- Other investments: A friend's start-up, the few crazy things you've done and so on.

Use joint bank accounts: Get at least one joint account with your spouse. In a joint account, either person can operate the account. In a single account, someone else will not be allowed to operate it; they'll have to transfer the account's balance to the next of kin first.

Set up nominees: For bank accounts, mutual funds and demat accounts, you can set up a nominee. A nominee is a person that the account will be transferred to in the event of your death. A nominee is not the legal heir of the proceeds, he or she is required to transfer the proceeds to the actual legal heir. But that is easier done with a family member, than with a bank. If you don't have a nominee, the bank will require a complex set of documentation in order to transfer money after your death, even if it's clear who your legal heirs are. Don't let your family get tangled up in this: Ensure your accounts have nominees.

Tell your spouse: You need to inform your spouse or a close family member about how much money you have and where it's stored. This is so obvious, but often neglected, and I've personally seen many situations where people haven't done any of this. I can tell you this: You don't want to be trying to tell someone about your financial life when you're struggling to survive inside an intensive care unit (ICU).

Keep key contacts: If you have an insurance agent, a financial adviser, or even a deeply trustworthy friend, please ensure the contact details of such a person are available to your family.

Revisit this info every quarter: Once a quarter, get yourself a tall drink and review the above information. If you're like me, you'll remember new things every time. A YouTube channel you once created. A little something you owe a friend. Another credit card you applied for. All the info you have helps, and if you keep a running note on how life has been for the last quarter, it'll serve as a good thing to relook every few years.

Write a will: A will can be on a piece of paper. A simple

> I, ………………….. daughter of ……………….., resident of ………………….., hereby revoke all my previous Wills and declare that this is my last Will, which I make on this ……. (Date) …………………
>
> My Date of Birth is …………..
>
> I declare that I am in good health and possess a sound mind. This Will is made by me without any persuasion or coercion and out of my own independent decision only
>
> My spouse's name is ………….. born on ……….
> I leave behind the following assets
>
> 1. House no ……… located at ……………….
> 2. Mutual funds, jewellery, cash, bank accounts, ppf accounts and shares in certain companies
>
> All the assets owned by me are self-acquired properties. I have full right and absolute power over these assets.
>
> I hereby bequeath all my properties, whether movable or immovable, whatsoever and wheresoever, to my spouse………..
> IN WITNESS WHEREOF I have hereunto set my hands on this …………(date) at ……………….(place).
>
> SIGNATURE

Signed by above ....(name) as her last Will and Testament, in our presence, and has understood perfectly and approved the contents and admits us as witnesses

1. Witness 1
2. Witness 2

This is simple, but if you need more complexity, remember that I'm not a lawyer, so you want to hire one.

Note: You can only will away property you own. If you have inherited any property, you can't will it away. You can sell it and then use the proceeds to buy something else, which you can then will to whoever you like.

Also note that Indian law is peculiar. So depending on which area you live in, which religion you belong to, or what peculiar situation you may be in, the rules will be different. Importantly, if you own property in, say, West Bengal and you live in Bengaluru (Karnataka), two sets of rules may apply.

Sometimes, however, you will need to be the one doing the transition. This could be a friend or a family member who passed away, and you're now being asked to help. This is when you need to do a few things.

Identify the assets: This is complex, if the person has left no records. You can use the person's phone to check SMS logs for messages from banks, and then connect with the banks to find out more details. You can also check the person's emails to see if there are loans, bank accounts, etc.

Everyone who has a demat account or a mutual fund will have their details in NSDL or CDSL, the core depositories in India.

Both provide something called a consolidated account statement (CAS) downloadable from their websites, if you provide a PAN number. You can use this to cross-verify what they own. Some insurance policies may also be available in such reports.

Physical assets are where you will need to see the items – a car, a house, or gold. You must find the ownership documentation here physically.

Plan the transfer: For all accounts that have nominees, you must identify the nominees and have them take possession of the accounts. Then the money and proceeds can be transferred to the legal heirs.

Some people may not leave a nominee in their accounts. For them, based on how much money is involved, you might need to work to build the following documents:

- If they have left a will, then the will must be **probated**, a concept that allows a court to say: Yes, indeed, this person has left a will and we will not distribute the assets around. Some places will charge a fee as a percentage of the assets, in order to probate the will (usually with an upper cap) and some places may not require a probate (such as Delhi).
- If there's no will, then for smaller amounts (typically less than a few lakh) you might obtain a **legal heirship certificate.** This is a certificate given by a local registrar stating who the legal heirs are. Along with this, the bank or mutual fund will demand an affidavit and indemnity bond to release the proceeds of the accounts.
- For larger amounts, where there is no will, you will need a **succession certificate**. This will need you to go to a civil court, and prove that the legal heirs are indeed the only ones (you may have to place an advertisement in a newspaper, etc.).

With the probated will, a legal heirship certificate or a succession certificate, you will need to contact every bank, every mutual fund or every demat service provider separately to effect the transfer to the appropriate legal heirs.

Note here that you no longer have to do this for each company you own shares in, if they are in the demat account. A single application to the demat provider is enough. (Similarly, if you own mutual funds in the demat account, you needn't approach the mutual funds, just transfer the demat account's holdings).

Claim insurance policies: You will need to claim insurance policies. Usually policies have a nomination, so all you might need is a death certificate.

Clear the loans: If people have loans on a house, they might have an insurance policy backing the loan. This allows the loan to be paid, and any excess amount refunded to the family. If not, you'll have to find a way to pay the loan (or forfeit the assets).

A quick note here: if there is a personal loan which is not secured by an asset, there is no need for the legal heir to pay for it. Car loans and home loans are secured. But a personal loan is not. However, note that if the person who dies leaves behind some assets which are transferred to an heir, then the lender can go to court requesting recovery from the estate of the person. This can complicate matters, so have the legal heirs clear the loan if there are assets.

In general, this process is not kind on anyone. So we need to make it easier for everyone involved, where we can. I really hope none of this has to happen to you, or to your family, but you can prepare yourself for the worst with the steps mentioned above. It is when you're well prepared that you can enjoy life a little more, in the confidence that should something happen, you'll leave things in the clear, financially.

Resources

Let's look at various resources that investors can use for their research and investment.

Mutual fund information

valueresearchonline.com	Value research is where you get information on all mutual funds in India. Shows returns, expense ratio, comparison with other funds
Moneycontrol, ET Money, etc.	Websites containing information on mutual funds, trailing
Mutual fund websites like SBImf.com, hdfcmf.com	Sites of the asset managers that run the mutual funds, with regular disclosures of portfolio, unit prices and other things

Buying mutual funds online

You can use the following websites to purchase or sell your funds online:

Start-ups: Kuvera, Groww, Paytm Money	Allow you to buy 'Direct' mutual funds onlne
Distributors: Scripbox, Fundsindia, Wealthy.in	Only allow 'Regular' mutual funds but some have nice tooling and product baskets

Brokers: Zerodha Coin, Angel Broking, ICICI Direct, Sharekhan	All brokerage websites that allow you to buy regular funds (only Zerodha allows Direct). Some of them will keep your funds in your demat account
mfuonline.com	Mutual Fund Utility – a company that is set up by all mutual funds together – allows you to purchase funds online
RTAs: camsonline.com and mfs.kfintech.com/	These companies are the underlying registrars and allow you to login and transact directly from their website. Only funds that they service can be bought here
Websites of the actual fund houses: Just search for IDFC, ICICI, HDFC, Nippon, etc. with the word 'mutual fund' at the end	Allow you to buy only the funds from their own offering. However, this assures you better control and service

Stock fundamentals

screener.in	Great site containing 10-year financials. You can also screen for stocks that meet your favourite criteria – like low P/E but great growth, etc.
trendlyne.com	Stock analysis site that also contains information on conference calls, transcripts and so on
tijori.in	Information on sectors, and many sector-specific information and data visualized in an easy-to-understand way
investing.com and barchart.com	Charts and international listed stocks and bonds

Planning your financial life

plan. capitalmindwealth.com	Our site that helps you plot goals and build your personal financial plan including for retirement, child's education, etc. (Disclosure: this is my company's site)
Online intermediaries such as Groww, Kuvera, Kotak, etc.	Basic calculators for personal finance and retirement

Pretty much the end

The point is, investing isn't simple, easy or a cakewalk. It's complicated, but so is life (and FB relationships) and we need to find a way to live and be happy anyhow. Just because some things about investing seem intimidating doesn't mean it cannot enrich your life.

There are things about my car that intimidate me, such as some orange-coloured icon that looks like someone wants to water their flowers, blinking away noisily. But I don't stop driving my car because of this weird thing I don't understand.

You don't stop walking on footpaths just because someone tells you the chances of pedestrians dying in an accident are greater than the chances of a driver dying. You don't stop eating because somewhere, sometime, one guy choked on his biryani.

You don't do these things because life isn't worth living if you can't ever have biryani. You might as well take the chance that it will take more than flavoured rice to kill you. You do that when you walk across the street. You do that because you know life isn't a bed of roses, but you can get by.

Investing is just like that. There's market manipulation, yes. There are times when the market is overstretched. There are times when you lose money, maybe a lot of money. But if you stay invested longer, you'll make it up. There are times when you get the sinking feeling that the company you really love, that makes those soaps and those shampoos and fancy deodorants, decides to double the royalty it pays its foreign parent, gypping the domestic shareholders, including you.

This can't deter you from investing in total. Get your allocation right, mixing high-risk and low-risk assets in the way that works for you. Get the diversification right between countries, and between different sectors.

Figure out who you are – a strong fundamentals-based investor, a price-based 'technical' investor, or simply a person who prefers to stay passive because, man, you have better things to do with your life.

In the end, you have to remember the famous two steps from Larry Hite:

If you don't bet, you can't win.
If you lose all your chips, you can't bet.

Stay alive. Plan for what you must be. Be who you are. And don't forget to live it up and enjoy yourself spending some of that wealth you'll end up with.

STOCKS

These things called shares

Of shares and stock markets

If you're wondering about these things called 'shares' or 'stocks', and how these affect your life, here goes.

The concept of shares

Let's say I get into a deal with a friend, Anup, and we start a company named Brouhaha Pvt. Ltd. We decide to split the initial investment 50–50. We need Rs 10 lakh to start up, so I put in Rs 5,00,000 and so does Anup.

Now we split this investment into 'shares'. Each share has a 'face value' of Rs 10, and so, each of us gets 50,000 shares. In total, the company has now 'issued' 1,00,000 shares of face value of Rs 10, which means our investment consists of 'equity' capital of Rs 10 lakh divided into 1,00,000 shares.

We have a great marketing strategy (this is wish fulfilment after all!) and the company grows quickly. We earn Rs 10 crore in profits. The total number of shares remains 1,00,000. This means we have an equal share of the profits and on a per-share basis, we have earned Rs 1000 per share (Rs 10 crore divided by 1,00,000 shares).

Then we decide we need cash to expand, and we'll want another Rs 60 crore to allow us to grow even faster. We can do several things. One is, go to a bank to borrow the cash. Another, ask other people to invest in the business. We decide to do the latter.

But who will give us Rs 60 crore? We can try and find a rich individual, or company. Or we can 'go public', meaning we ask a LOT of people to become small shareholders. Each of them can invest relatively small amounts. In return, we will issue shares to them. Again, we go with the latter option.

But will we sell them the fresh shares at the face value of Rs 10? Obviously not – the company has earned Rs 10 crore profits on that initial Rs 10 lakh capital we put in. Plus there are other assets owned by the business. So the value of the company is much more now!

The exact price we can charge is a matter of 'valuation'. Typically, this valuation is set on the basis of how fast you expect to grow your company in the future. One key valuation tool is called the Price to Earnings ratio or P/E ratio, which is a multiple of net profits.

For example, if you earn Rs 10 in profits per share and you price a share at Rs 100, the P/E ratio is 10. Again, the faster you expect to grow, the higher the P/E ratio your shares may be valued at. We'll explain how the logic works, later.

Let's say we expect a Price to Earnings ratio (P/E) of 15 on our last twelve months worth of earnings. This is a conservative value we believe we can get, given our track record. We talk to investment bankers and decide to go public with an initial public offer (IPO) valuing the company at Rs 150 crore (Rs 10 crore profit x 15 P/E ratio) to raise the Rs 60 crore we need.

That means those 1,00,000 shares that Anup and I own

would now be valued at Rs 150 crore. That's a value of Rs 15,000 per share. This is a big number and people would be wary about investing in shares priced at Rs 15,000 each.

> *Note:* It is a little irrational to be intimidated by the high price of a share. A share at 15 times earnings might be at Rs 15,000 per share, but a different company could be at 30 times earnings, but only at Rs 90 per share. The price is measured relative to earnings, not as an absolute number.

The profits over the last few years have been accumulated as 'Reserves' in our balance sheet. So, our company has Rs 10 crore in reserves but only Rs 10 lakh as capital. The 'Net Worth' of the company is Rs 10.1 crore. We now decide to issue more shares to ourselves as 'bonus shares', reducing the reserves and increasing the capital. This is a technical accounting term – it moves money from one entry (Reserves) to another (Paid-up Capital), without changing the Net Worth. It just gives the shareholders fresh shares with no extra added value. If you like, we're using the accumulated profits to 'buy' those new shares, even though the cash itself stays with the company.

We do what's called a '99:1 bonus' – every shareholder (just Anup and I at this point) gets 99 shares for every one share we already owned. This increases the total number of shares from 1,00,000 to 1 crore, again all at a 'face value' of Rs 10. So, Anup and I are now owners of 50 lakh shares each. And each share is worth Rs 150 according to our reckoning (Rs 150 crore total value of the company, divided by one crore shares)

So since Rs 150 per share is a more palatable price for a small shareholder, now we must calculate how many shares are needed to be issued to raise Rs 60 crore. To get that Rs 60 crore, we will issue 40 lakh new shares (each at a price of Rs 150 and a face value of Rs 10). Effectively, we are diluting our ownership. We will continue to own 50 lakh shares each, but other shareholders will own 40 lakh shares between them. Collectively, Anup and I go from owning 100 per cent of the business, to owning only 70 per cent. That's in exchange for Rs 60 crore, which we can use to grow the business.

Having carried out this accounting magic of giving ourselves a bonus, we go for an IPO. We will ask anyone who wants to own a share of our business to pay Rs 150. Post-IPO, the company will have a total of 1.4 crore shares (1 crore earlier and 40 lakh freshly issued shares) and it will be listed on a stock exchange. Anyone can then buy and sell our shares.

This is a dream example. So let's say the company's shares list at Rs 150, but because the company is expected to grow fast, the price zooms up to Rs 200 per share on listing.

Now, let's say a person named Sarath wants to become a shareholder. The company has got all the money it needs from the IPO. So no further shares are going to be issued. But Sarath can buy shares from the stock exchange. He buys a share at Rs 200. So he's willing to pay more than the IPO price to own a share because he thinks the company will do well.

The person who sold the share to Sarath got it in the IPO, at Rs 150. Now he makes a profit of Rs 50. Later, as the company starts doing well, and more people want the shares, the share price continues to go up.

So let's say Sarath sells it to someone else later, at an even higher price of say 250. The company doesn't really get affected because that money isn't coming to the company. But the personal net worth of shareholders (Anup, me, others who own the share) goes up because the share price goes up.

Why does the share price go up? The answer is: Perceived value. I may think a company is worth Rs 1 crore, but someone else thinks it's worth Rs 2 crore. When my shares reach my valuation I sell, but someone else thinks it's a good deal and buys.

To organize such buying and selling, there are commercial 'stock exchanges'. BSE and NSE are the two biggest exchanges in India, though there are other, smaller exchanges. An exchange provides a common marketplace for people to trade shares.

The sales happen on an auction format on computer screens: Buyers 'bid' for shares at the price they are willing to pay, and sellers 'ask' for a price from buyers. Exchanges match these prices and the shares are transferred along with payments. 'Brokers' facilitate these trades, and you pay a fee as 'brokerage'. Part of this fee goes to the stock exchange.

How do you buy stocks? What happens when you do?

There are some formalities involved before you can participate in this process of trading shares. Once that process is complete you can trade shares at lightning speed.

Here's the basic paperwork (actually digital since it can all be done online) you need to be able to buy stocks in India:

- You have to open a 'demat' (short for dematerialized) account, and a trading account.
- The demat account is where you store the stocks you own. Stocks are traded via digital certificates, not paper shares.
- A trading account is held with the broker through whom you trade. In general, when you sell, you transfer stocks to your broker, and he transfers stocks to your demat account when you buy.

- To ease this process, you usually hold the demat account with the same service provider with whom you have the trading account. This is usually the broker, who allows you to buy, sell and store shares, for a fee. (It's fine to hold several demat accounts and use several brokers too but let's not complicate things at this stage.)
- Does this mean that if the broker goes bust, you lose all your shares?
- The answer (after a bunch of brokers went bust) is no.
- Actually the digital certificates of the shares are recorded at a 'Depository'. There are two big-daddy depositories, NSDL (National Securities Depository Limited) and CDSL (Central Depository Services Limited).
- If your broker shuts shop, your shares are still held in one or the other of the depositories (they talk to each other) and that keeps you safer.

The broker will have a website where you can create an account, and buy or sell shares. You may need to give a power of attorney to operate the account digitally at speed.

Now, you need to transfer money to the broker in order to buy shares. In the old days, you could buy now and pay later. To avoid defaults, when customers buy but don't pay, brokers take some money upfront and hold it in a customer's ledger. You can use that money to pay for your stocks any time.

Buying and selling is about placing orders with your broker. Stock markets are open for a limited time, five days of the week apart from special sessions at the Budget, on Diwali and so on. The exchanges are shut on weekends. So you can only trade during 'market hours'.

Once you've got the paperwork done and opened your accounts you're ready to move on towards the next part – and the more interesting part – of the business:

- What do I buy?
- How much?
- At what price?
- What should I sell?
- How do I figure out if all of this is making me money?

Nothing comes easy, so I'll try and explain how all this works by telling my own story.

How I started investing in stocks

My investing journey

This is going to be a long story. I'm going to tell you how I started investing in stocks and how it progressed.

My father and his friends would always be discussing some stock or the other. So I was aware of the existence of the stock market for the most part of my life but I didn't know anything more about it.

He made me read out the stock prices from the newspaper once in a while, which is how I knew that prices also actually changed. This was boring for me, as a child – who wants to be involved with reading out boring numbers as a kid?

But this apparently seemed to make people money. You could buy at 100. And that thing you bought could go to 200. And you'd make a profit! As a kid, I mean it didn't matter what that thing was – I mean, it could be potatoes and it would be just as exciting (you can buy and sell potatoes too on commodity exchanges!).

Some of these stock market concepts did not make sense. Stocks went up or down for no reason, apparently, other than that one more day had passed. It seemed to me like someone was getting a report card every single day.

To me, making money meant working and getting paid. I went to an engineering college – KREC (now NIT) Surathkal on the western coast of Karnataka. We had a beach and 350 acres of a wonderful campus, and in that, I found a whole new life. College is where I discovered what I wanted to be. A computer engineer. I learnt about programming and technology. I was hooked. I would stay up nights learning about coding in different languages, about how you could make a computer do whatever you wanted.

At this stage of my life, money was about sustenance; if you had money, you'd go to the dhaba (there was exactly one) and have a meal. If you didn't, you'd eat the watery stuff they'd serve in the mess. And if things got really bad, there were the food vendors near the college gate that were happy to give you a little credit.

College, though, did present some opportunities of making money. A bunch of people got hired at TCS. They needed to pass a test on COBOL and C++. I knew something about the two languages, so I taught this in a class and charged a fee.

Then there were competitions. In college, I discovered a talent I had no idea about. I could speak on stage, impromptu. Also, my group project was impressive enough to get us into inter-college competitions. Both these efforts ended up making me and my teammates some prize money. The common link: You do some work, you make some money.

After college, I worked at a couple of jobs before starting my own business. This was the dream for me right through – to be my own boss. It is quite in fashion now. But in 1998 it was considered a little below suicide, on the scale of things people shouldn't do.

The idea was simple as far as I was concerned. Being my own boss gave me the freedom to do big or great things, and to build a business around that. And then, I thought it would help me build an asset that might continue to pay me something even if I stopped working.

Think about it. You work on a job, and you get paid a salary. You stop working, the salary stops. But that's crazy, because a lot of the things you helped to build will continue to serve the business you worked for.

It is only crazy because you owned nothing. You sold your time, and got money in return. Owning a company is different – you work, and the business will make money when you work. But if you grow it well, you can hire people to do the work, and at some point, even if you stop doing any work yourself, your ownership earns money anyhow.

Note: I know that there are many companies where you may not ever actually work and still continue to earn a salary – it's called a sinecure. This was not information available to me at the time I joined the workforce. I was always too ambitious to have taken such a sinecure, I think.

My idea in starting a company was to earn through ownership, while someone else did the grunt work. Even if, for the first few years, I did the grunt work myself. I was lucky enough to have friends who felt the same way, and we teamed up and started a company with four computers and a list of prospective customers we could sell to.

It was a lot of work, of course. My first contract was to teach Java for Rs 3000 per day. For a week. And I didn't know anything about Java! But I was 22 and at that age, over a weekend, you could learn anything. And I did learn Java, at least enough to teach a basic course.

From there, we built cash flow through the training business. Meanwhile, two of my partners decided to build an accounting software to target the users of Tally, a popular software that is used by a lot of companies. Tally had some flaws and limitations – it wasn't usable by different people in a network, for example, and we thought we could provide competition.

I was involved primarily in building out the cash flow business – which scaled from training to custom product development for customers all over the world. Slowly we hired more people and grew the cash flow business.

We did some work on an accounting software for the US as well. It was during this time that I started to get interested in accounting. The concepts were complex but we had to look at public company accounts to understand how certain things were done. It was fascinating.

The mad FOMO

It's early 2000. The tech boom has gone through the roof. The Sensex is making new highs, nearly every day. The year 1999 had been an insane year. The Sensex started at 3000 in January 1999 and by May, it touched 4000 – a 33 per cent jump. It then went even further – crossing 5000 by the end of the year, for a 64 per cent move in 12 months. And in the first two months of 2000, it went up – hold your breath – to 6000, and that was a 20 per cent return in two months. This looked like a juggernaut that would never stop.

I wanted to be in the stock market. I didn't want to miss out. And this was the first time I had any money. My startup was profitable enough for me to pay myself a salary.

I could not understand why tech companies were going up. This was a crazy time. A Wipro would just double on the conjecture of a bonus. Every second company inserted 'infotech' in its name just to get the attention of shareholders.

We had to stand in line for an IPO of a new technology fund launched by ICICI Mutual Fund. I placed all my savings, a valuable Rs 10,000, into this fund buying 1000 units at Rs 10 a unit. (That's roughly the equivalent of Rs 35,000 in 2021 money which gives you an insight into inflation by the way.)

But within six months, the dotcom bubble had gone bust. By December 2000, the Sensex was back at 4000. From the heights, it was 33 per cent down. Technology, though, was down a lot more than the broad index – my Rs 10 IPO price units were trading at Rs 2 a unit. I had lost 80 per cent of my capital!

I learnt a lesson. When you don't understand something, don't participate in it at the peak of a buying frenzy. And if you do get sucked in, learn to sell it fast. Because when you didn't get in knowing much, you should get out while the going is good.

You'll probably feel FOMO – the fear of missing out – at some time in your life. How could you miss the madness of the upside when everyone was making money? But the FOMO is the highest closest to the top.

What that experience actually taught me was – there's no point doing something because you're getting FOMO. There's got to be a better reason and a better way.

Broker reports and friendly tips

One thing that did happen during the dot-com boom was that people would send you 'tips' all the time. Brokerage reports of stocks that did well, with estimates of how well the stocks would do going forward.

I would get those as well, on email and on the early forms of instant messengers. This gave me the feeling that people knew what they were talking about, and that I should probably listen to them. Some tips would be quite detailed, with strong reasons given why a stock would do well.

In the early 2000s, the first online brokerages also launched. Charging only 0.5 per cent or so, these were the 'discount' brokers at the time, since everyone else was charging a minimum of 1 per cent of order value per trade. Discount brokers could be used via a computer – you could place an order when you liked, without needing to speak to a human being. I found that fascinating, and you could easily transfer money online too (or drop a cheque in the broker's account).

This also gave me access to broker research, where they would have deeper analysis about each stock (or so I thought!) and estimates of how they would do in the future. I had a rudimentary understanding of financial accounts at the time. I cared only about one thing – do these people think profits will go up? Undoubtedly, they always did!

I would buy stocks. And then wait. And then I'd get another report. I'd buy that too. By this time, I started to feel something was wrong. If there was a new stock every week, how much should I be putting on each stock? Would I end up with 100 stocks in two years? So I should have a maximum of 1 per cent per stock?

There wasn't much of an answer to those questions. I realized something else as well. If a stock was doing badly the brokers would conveniently remove the stock from their coverage universe. Saying we don't track this stock any more. Oh, then I should sell? But the answer to that question was also: 'We don't track this stock any more!'

This was similar to friendly tips. They'd tell you to buy. If the stock went up, you'd get calls saying I told you so. If the stock fell, they'd ignore it. They would send you a new 'tip' every day or two, and invariably one stock or the other was doing well, so there was always an I-told-you-so somewhere in the picture.

And then, they'd tell you to take a profit as soon as there was one. So you didn't sell when the stock lost money, but you always were supposed to sell when the stock went up? The fear was that it would fall again. But inherently, something felt wrong with this logic. If the stocks were so good, why would they fall so much that you couldn't hold on?

Meanwhile, the portfolio my mother inherited from my father was starting to do very well. In the eight years after 1997, the stocks in that portfolio saw major falls and rises, and yet, the survivors – there were only a few, as I noted in the introduction – were going up slowly and steadily. What was different about those stocks? L&T, Hero Honda (now Motocorp) and Ranbaxy were doing well.

It dawned on me that either I should get serious about understanding how stocks worked, or I should do something else. The concept of relying on tips was useless. You needed a better approach that you could track in a manner that made more sense.

So I went down the rabbit hole of fundamentals.

Deep fundamentals

Every listed company is required to reveal its profit and loss statement every quarter. This concept of informing shareholders was new to Indian markets. The general idea earlier was: Listen, if you care we might send you a report once a year. But the quarterlies did help you understand how the business was doing.

My go-to strategy was simple. Is a company's revenue growing? Check. Are profits growing? Check. What's the Profit after Tax per share? Rs x, growing at, say, 15 per cent a year. Ok, is the stock price less than 15x? If yes, then buy the share, otherwise don't.

This sounds utterly simplistic but it's an interesting approach. The profit per share is called the EPS (earning per share). The stock price divided by the EPS is the **Price to Earning Ratio** or the P/E as mentioned earlier.

The idea was:
- If a company makes Rs 10 in profits per share and grows profits 15 per cent a year, I should pay a maximum of Rs 150 per share (the percentage 15 X EPS of 10).
- Think of it this way: If it maintains the same growth rate, then the Rs 10 in year 1 will become Rs 11.5 in year 2, Rs 13.2 in year 3 and so on until it is Rs 35 per share in year 10.
- In 10 years, the profit, added up, would be more than Rs 200 per share. That's a good return for a Rs 150 investment. And if this trend continues the stock would continue to have growth in the future.
- If the stock continues to have a P/E of 15, the stock price would rise to Rs 527 in 10 years, which is a 3x return. If the share price has stayed the same (unlikely given the strong growth), I've still got a return of 9 per cent in paper profits. If

the company paid dividends I've received some of that cash. If it didn't pay dividends, this could be notional but I hope the growth will be reflected in share price.
- A savvy investor might also compare this return (earnings as per cent of price) with the return from a fixed deposit. You want a premium return from shares compared to FDs because of the greater risk. But I wasn't that savvy at the time.

This is as simple as it gets in terms of logic. But I realized there were issues with this approach.

Dangerous cycles

Some companies were cyclical. They would grow well for four years, and struggle for the next four. You couldn't extrapolate the growth rate easily. Cyclicals had to be dealt with differently.

In 2006, for example, the steel cycle was starting to go up and Tata Steel decided to take a big plunge. It bought a massive global giant, Corus, for billions of dollars. The idea was right, but the timing was not. The steel upcycle lasted another year or so before it plunged downwards and that took Tata Steel down with it. Buying Corus meant taking on some really nasty debt, and also a lot of union hassles with factories located in developed countries (the UK and Holland). The idea of just shutting down plants wasn't palatable, and the Tata group kept putting duct tape on the bleeding for a long time. Result: A stock that went nowhere for 10 long years.

A similar trend was visible in 2010. In stocks that made plastic film. You know, the kind that potato chips are packaged in. That 'thin film' is made of BOPET, which stands for bioxially oriented polyethylene terephthalate. This is information that is largely useless for most of you, but see what 'deep fundamentals" do! Anyhow . . .

BOPET manufacturing was changing. Some of the largest plants around the world decided to either shut down permanently, or temporarily for repairs. The supply reduced. But people were still eating potato chips by the truckloads. Therefore, demand remained the same.

The economics theory is that when supply reduces and demand is the same, there's a mismatch. Prices will go up. BOPET prices were going up. Massively. Some companies made BOPET, and their margins were going through the roof. Because all it takes to make this is a petroleum-based monomer as raw material, and thin film extruded through a machine. Your fixed costs remain much the same. Your output sales prices are going up. Super-normal margins occurred, and companies made big profits.

A few companies in India were benefiting from this change. UFlex and Jindal Poly Films were two of them, and they made enormous profits for a short period of time. However, if the process of making thin film only involves a machine and some raw material, anyone can do it. And if you're earning super-normal margins, a lot of people will try to get into the game.

Plus, customers started to slowly replace BOPET with BOPP, another type of thin film which did not have this supply–demand mismatch. Once the temporary shutdowns ended, and more people entered the business, the supply of BOPET resumed and there was a migration partially into BOPP. But people weren't eating potato chips any more. So the supply-demand mismatch normalized.

Jindal Poly's price shot up from Rs 400 to Rs 1400 in two months. Imagine. A 250 per cent return – the kind of money that makes you think you should just sell your house and buy the stock. And the stock was at a relatively decent P/E of just 17 times earnings at top price of Rs 1400 per share, when it was growing earnings at 400 per cent. Sounds like a buy on the P/E to growth equation? Sure!

But the cyclical nature of the business would teach you a lesson. In a few months, the stock crashed 75 per cent. Then, it took another 11 years – till 2021 – to cross the highs made in 2010.

Another example: The graphite electrode madness. China was reeling under smog in 2017 when it decided that it must stop running steel furnaces that burn iron ore (using coal) and produce steel while releasing extreme amounts of smoke. China had steel mills on such massive scales that its steel production capacity was more than that of the next six countries combined (India is #4).

The shutting down of basic oxygen furnaces meant that there was less steel to export for China. Other countries, which couldn't match the Chinese steel production efficiency and cost (and lack of pollution controls), started to see margins reviving in their own steel plants. Except, most of the steel plants outside China were of a different type, using electric arc furnaces (EAFs).

Steel can be made in two ways: You take iron ore (which is iron oxide), and burn out the oxide at very high temperatures in a basic oxygen furnace (BOF) and you're left with iron. Combine that with carbon (by burning coal) and you get steel. This is a polluting process, but countries like India and China that have had scant regard for their citizens' health use this process widely.

The other way is to take steel that's already out there – in cars, in other scrap – and melt it at very high temperatures. For that, you use electrodes which form an electric arc. The heat produced takes temperatures to 4000 degrees Celsius. These electrodes are made of graphite – a form of carbon that can survive at those temperatures and continue to conduct electricity. This is far less polluting than the BOF route.

When China stopped BOF based steel, there were EAF plants, in China and worldwide, that took the opportunity to make steel. Their demand: Graphite electrodes. When demand suddenly goes up, supply takes time to adjust. Graphite electrode manufacturing plants are not easy to set up. The largest were a Japanese company and an American one, but two Indian companies also stood out. The Bangur-led Graphite India, and HEG, another electrode player.

Electrode prices rose dramatically. The economics were such that a 100 per cent rise in electrode prices could be covered by a mere 1 per cent to 2 per cent increase in steel prices; the leverage of input costs to output price was so high. Graphite India's stock price went from Rs 150 in mid-2017 to Rs 1100 in August 2018. A rise of over 600 per cent in a year. This is the stuff of dreams. But after that, the stock fell 70 per cent the next year, when the cycle was complete.

When playing a cycle you need to understand the points at which margins will compress and the stock will fall. Typically, stock prices fall way before any of us realize the situation is changing for the worse. By the time Graphite India's December 2018 quarter results were out – where you could see the margins drop for the first time in four quarters – the price had corrected 50 per cent from the top.

A lot of industries are cyclical. The cycles can be long or short. To truly understand cyclicals, you have to be on top of the industry and you need to learn to exit before prices crash in the down-cycle.

Great companies seem expensive, but can you pay too much?

There's another problem with the P/E ratio. Sometimes a company seems expensive when measured by the pure P/E ratio. This is because they've built a franchise that works brilliantly even in the worst of times. Or (and this may come to much the same thing) investors are happy to pay a higher price for a really good management team.

For the longest time, FMCG companies – those that sell toothpaste, soaps, shampoos and so on – were super-expensive measured by the P/E ratio, compared to the growth they were showing. In 2021, Colgate was valued at 43 times earnings (P/E) even though it had only doubled profits in 10 years. (That's only 7 per cent per year.)

When I asked around, I was told various things that 'explained' why they remained super-expensive:

- These are great world-class companies. Like Colgate, or Nestlē. You pay a premium for that kind of company and governance.
- Such companies have no debt. They have managed to build a franchise that needs no more cash additions and the cash flows they have generated have paid for any debt in the past. This makes them more resilient – and in effect, a cash machine.
- These companies also have a strong brand for a moat. Now that sounds interesting as a philosophy, but great brands do fail. Like Xerox. Or Polaroid. Or Kodak. The market may 'think' a brand is great, but it usually is not as bulletproof as it seems. In India, household name brands like Kingfisher Airlines, Jet Airways and so on have failed spectacularly.

Buying companies when they are expensive can seem like a good strategy if you believe, strongly, that the companies will never fail, and will always be valued at that much. This may not be the case, though, even for the best brands in the world.

Horror story alert

There was a group of American stocks called the Nifty Fifty in the early 1970s. These were a set of 50 companies that were 'bluechip', the best of the stock market. It was said that these stocks were only to be bought, not sold. No matter what the price!

The story that they told us about the expensive Indian FMCG companies in the 2000s was the same for the US Nifty Fifty in the 1970s: Low debt, strong balance sheets, great brands, etc. In 1972, the average P/E ratio of these Nifty Fifty stocks was 42, when the S&P 500 itself had a P/E of 19. Polaroid was traded at 91 times earnings, and McDonald's at 86 times.

Eventually the US stocks collapsed after a strong rise in crude oil prices, and rising inflation that hit interest rates. Some of those 50 stocks had fallen 60 per cent or more, from their peaks, by 1974. Even 10 years later, after growing earnings more than three times, this group of stock was up just 1.7 per cent a year. However, some of those stocks, McDonald's included, went on to give stellar returns over the next thirty years – McDonald's itself returned an average of 12 per cent a year for forty years if you held it that long.*

The problem is that sometimes we don't quite have that much time. If you buy a stock only at its highs and don't add more

---

*https://www.ft.com/content/3ae0eda2-0116-330d-b6e0-663d35fa456d

when it falls, you're going to take a long time to recover your investment even if it's doing well. Great businesses are likely to give better returns if you invest regularly in them, adding more shares when they fall, rather than investing at one time and forgetting about it.

I learnt this lesson in a strange way – by avoiding the 'high P/E' stocks and realizing the high P/E in some cases was an illusion. Solid balance sheets were good enough for longer term growth in some cases even if the stock seemed expensive. But in other cases I realized, a high P/E was an indication of over-enthusiasm and the stocks in question never recovered after a steep fall.

The balance sheet is more important than profit

Profits are great, and perhaps the most important reason to run a business. However, it may be that the profits shown on the profit and loss (P&L) statements hide certain important information which is only revealed in the balance sheet.

I learnt quickly that the balance sheet is the boring thing. It shows much more useful information but it's harder to understand. It tells you about debt levels, what kind of money sits in inventory and working capital, and other things such as investments, liabilities, reserves, etc.

Let's look at just one example of where the balance sheet was more important than the P&L. A real estate company called DLF was all the vogue in 2007. The founder and his family had prospered as Gurugram grew wildly beyond anybody's imagination, and DLF's apartment complexes were gobbled up by new residents. Alongside, DLF had set up incredibly large office spaces, which they apparently owned and rented to large corporations. DLF would regularly announce huge profits and the stock was even included in the Nifty index (which is an index of India's 50 largest listed companies), and extremely popular.

Yet, the balance sheet showed a serious problem. DLF would not actually receive rents from commercial property. They would sell the commercial property to a privately held company called DLF Assets. This was majority owned by the promoters of DLF. So the listed company DLF sells the commercial property to DLF assets for a price, say Rs x.

But the buyer doesn't actually pay anything to DLF! And therein lies the rub. DLF Assets said it owed DLF money. So DLF, would say we sold Rs x worth of commercial real estate. This accounts for revenues and it registers as profit on the profit and loss statement. But since DLF hasn't got the money yet, it would be called a 'receivable', from DLF Assets.

Receivables are shown only on the balance sheet. So DLF got revenue on the books to show as profits to its shareholders every quarter. But it didn't get any cash. The rentals and whatever other incomes would go to DLF Assets and into the pockets of the promoters.

The receivables would keep growing, and so would the sales. Since there was no cash received, DLF would have to keep borrowing to survive, despite making record revenues.

Once the street figured this out, they asked the promoters why DLF Assets – their personal company – wasn't paying DLF, the listed company. The story goes that the promoters wanted to list DLF Assets in Singapore, and with the proceeds, pay the cash owed to DLF.

That didn't happen due to many reasons – a global financial crisis, a lack of interest in commercial real estate and so on.

So what happens next? DLF merges itself with DLF Assets,

cancelling the receivables and restating revenue for the past. Massive losses occur, and even in 2021, the price of the DLF share was lower than its listing price in 2007.

The balance sheet also has important data about a few things you might not notice otherwise. For instance, if a company is getting paid in advance for its services, and can delay payment to its suppliers for a few months, it effectively has some cash to burn.

Receivables minus payables plus inventory makes up working capital, which is the cash you need to keep your business running smoothly. If you have advances (that means low or zero receivables because you demand and get payment fast) but high payables (because your suppliers are willing to wait for payment), you may have negative working capital. For businesses, this is super-efficient use of their brand or power – and many great brands enjoy this, since they can afford to ask for upfront payment from distributors, while getting a credit period from their suppliers

Another interesting thing in the balance sheet is a whole set of return ratios. Assume a company makes Rs 100 in net profit. Does it do it on capital of Rs 500? Or Rs 10,000? Capital is simply the money that shareholders have invested in the business, plus any retained profits so far (retained means what the company hasn't paid back in dividends).

If it earns Rs 100 on a Rs 500 capital base, you have a 20 per cent 'return on equity' (ROE). A high ROE business is effectively telling you that the management can make great returns by sweating the cash they have.

You can still over-pay for a share, of course. Just because the business makes 20 per cent ROE doesn't mean you can pay 80 times earnings to buy it. That means if a company makes Rs 100 per share on a Rs 500 per share capital base, you can't pay

Rs 8,000 per share for it. Sometimes people do this, because they love the balance sheet more than anything else. This is a little like paying the price of a Mercedes for a sturdy, reliable Maruti Baleno.

Divi's Lab and Amazon are other interesting examples of companies that weren't easy to analyse because the good stuff was in the balance sheet.

Amazon kept showing losses for a long time. But this company never raised any fresh equity capital. This was perplexing – how can you lose money and still not need money to stay alive? The answer was: Cash flow. The company would generate cash, and instantly use it to create longer term assets, such as a server business, or develop tools like Alexa and Kindle. This ensured Amazon's profits were lower, or indeed negative, for a long time. However, the business didn't need to raise more cash! A look at the balance sheet and cash flow statement showed you that the cash generated was being pumped into longer term investments, and it was so much that Amazon simply didn't need to raise capital for the business to survive. Eventually the new investments became cash cows, and the profits showed up, more than a decade later.

Divi's Laboratories was a quiet little company that again raised capital only once, in 2003. That was what it needed to expand its manufacturing facility in Visakhapatnam, where it made 'Active Pharmaceutical Ingredients', the stuff that works in any drug. After that, it grew from putting its own cash flows back into the business. Companies that don't need to raise more money have strong balance sheets, even if their profit and loss statements don't yell that fact out at you.

Then again, there are banks, whose profits come from manipulating their balance sheets. Banks can make profits in many different ways. They give you loans, they get interest. They give you credit cards, they make money from joining fees, transaction charges to merchants and by interest if you delay payment. Then they can invest in things and make profits when the prices of those things go up. But loans can also run into default. If you have too many defaults, the street will punish that bank's stock price.

So banks will try to hide this away, and they can. A company can't pay? Oh, no problem, we'll just lend money to a sister concern of that company, which will route the money back to ensure the first company pays up. The sister concern's loan is a problem, but that's now three months away from being recognized as a bad loan, so the bank buys some time by this process of 'greening'.

A loan can also be muddled – instead of charging 9 per cent interest for three years, the bank says give me 3 per cent upfront, and take a loan at 8 per cent for three years instead. This increases current income (a 9 per cent loan would see income over the course of the loan as against an upfront fee that would reflect in a single quarter), and makes it difficult for shareholders to understand much.

The regulator (meaning the RBI) has tried to plug these loopholes, but bankers aren't giving up on this sort of jugglery just yet. Experienced investors learn to treat a bank's stated profits with caution and look for tells in entries like 'Provisions & Contingencies', where the bank is writing off bad loans.

In other cases, companies sometimes demand that they be allowed to lie to shareholders. Take the case of telecom companies, which took loans to buy equipment. These loans were in US dollars, so they had to repay in dollars.

But let's say a year later the rupee–dollar exchange rate has changed. The rupee has fallen. If one dollar was Rs 50 when the loan was taken, it became Rs 60 a year later. Technically if you had to repay a one-dollar debt, you would have to pay Rs 60 now, which is Rs 10 more than when you took the loan. This should be a Rs 10 loss for you (unless you are earning in dollars, or you have managed to hedge out the risk in some way).

Now telecom companies weren't doing either. They only had rupee revenues, and they thought the cost of hedging (by buying future dollars at today's price plus a little premium) was too high. So when the time came to recognize those losses, they cried foul – saying it wasn't their fault the rupee had fallen.

The authorities listened to them and allowed such loan repayments to happen 'silently'. If you bought equipment for $1 on a loan it would be recorded as an asset at Rs 50 (that day's conversion rate) on your books. The liability too – the loan – would be recorded at Rs 50. If the rupee fell to Rs 60, the asset would still be reflected at 50, so the liability side would show: Loan of Rs 60 and loss of Rs 10, which balances out.

Losses are bad, of course. So the company was allowed to say this: 'Oh, let's just say we bought the asset at Rs 60 instead, and the liability (loan) becomes Rs 60.' If you looked at just the profit and loss statement, you'd notice no change in this case. It was buried in the details of the balance sheet. This is a nice way to allow the business to keep hiding away what is really a true loss (if I earn in rupees and what I repay is Rs 60 where I would have repaid Rs 50 earlier, I do actually lose money).

The cash flow statement is another charming device. It's what tells you where the cash comes in and where it goes out. It is much more difficult to manipulate cashflows without committing outright fraud than concealing details in the P&L or Balance sheet. Experienced investors study cash flow statement (CFS) carefully. In cases like DLF as mentioned above, the company is 'highly profitable' but it's 'cash-flow negative', which is a red flag. A company like Amazon, on the other hand, was 'loss-making' but 'cash flow positive'.

Now consider a new beast called the Infrastructure Investment Trust (InvIT). This is a vehicle for grouping together infrastructure cash flows (like transmission lines where payment from the electricity commissions may stretch for 30 years) and allowing investors to take little pieces of these pool, called units. The InvIT effectively purchases the underlying transmission lines, for instance, and maintains them, and passes on all the money collected, minus costs, to the unitholders.

The profit and loss statement and the balance sheet are muddled – they will show some depreciation of the underlying assets, and the numbers might show a loss as well. The balance sheet, too, is not as relevant. The main thing here is the cash flow – how much money is coming in from the assets every month? This determines how much investors get paid. In such a case you would actually ignore the balance sheet and P&L, and instead focus on the cash flow statement.

The CFS gives you an idea of how well a company is generating cash. A company that makes a lot of profit but has to keep more and more of it stuck in working capital is inherently unhealthy, because that means the cash generated is not 'free' – it is needed to continue to run the business. The lack of free cash flow is not sometimes evident in one-off years, so you have to add up cash flows over years to understand the true nature of the business.

A retailer like D-Mart has a peculiar habit: It attempts to buy the real estate on which the D-Mart retail shops are located. This may seem like a terrible use of capital at a point when yields on commercial rents are just 4 per cent of the property value. But the point of doing this is not for today; it's for a future time, when rents go up. Owning such assets makes the balance sheet look bloated, and their profits relatively high, and the cash generated isn't that much. But a few years down the line, you might find that D-Mart gained in a big way from owning the assets, simply because they don't have to pay rent, and the real estate might be revalued upwards. They could even make a profit in selling that piece of land and buying something else that's cheaper. Valuing a D-Mart must account for this key difference that might add big numbers to margins tomorrow, even if they are subdued today. That's a long-term bet investors must evaluate.

As I came across these examples, I realized that investing was even more complicated than it looked. There was more hidden in the balance sheet than you could make out from just looking at revenue or profit. And companies had to reveal the balance sheet only twice a year (September and March).

It's complicated enough to track companies, the news and so on. And you had the added complexity of balance sheets, legally allowed manipulation and so on. Not so much fun. What if we just talked to management and heard their views?

Management and analyst commentary: Don't get married

Company managements may or may not be good at managing to run a business but they're usually suave, smooth-talking folks and great sales people. The problem is: As investors, we want to believe them, even when they're not being altogether truthful. In effect management becomes friends, and you can get too defensive about a company even when it's obviously doing something that's way off the charts.

Take, for example, the brilliant Rana Kapoor of Yes Bank. He was aggressive, charming and one of the smartest people in the business. Interview him at any time and he'd tell you the bank was growing, that they could raise capital when they wanted and that everything was awesome. Yes Bank did grow quickly and it was even included in the big stock indices.

Everything, however, wasn't awesome, and the RBI raised quite a few tough questions over multiple years about why Yes Bank wasn't actually recording bad loans the way it was required to. Eventually, the RBI flatly refused to allow Kapoor to remain the CEO and he had to resign. (Yes, the RBI has this power.)

The stock immediately fell 35 per cent. What changes for a national-level bank with over Rs 2,00,000 crore in assets if only the CEO changes? The answer wasn't apparent for a while, but it turned out that no one could really figure out how bad the situation was.

For four quarters, even with a new CEO in charge, the bank kept losing money. In December 2018, the RBI decided to step in strongly. It put the bank in a moratorium (which meant that it couldn't make any new loans and no one could withdraw their money beyond a small amount), brought in the State Bank of India as a rescuer, and asked (it's not really a request when the RBI 'asks') other banks to pitch in money for a bailout. The bank was rescued and it came out of the moratorium, but the stock price fell over 90 per cent from the top. And in fact, it was down more than 90 per cent from the stock price that prevailed even on the day Rana Kapoor was fired.

The takeaway: You don't want to believe management blindly, just because they sound nice. There are cautionary signs, lapses in governance and wilful ignorance that become apparent only in bad times.

When SEBI started to see issues with governance, it told auditors that it intended to hold them responsible if they didn't cross-verify data that management told them. In a few companies, the auditors resigned. Soon, it became evident that in some companies, the auditor was actually quite uncomfortable with the accounting processes, and given stronger oversight, they didn't want to ruin their own reputations.

News of this sort hit a company called Manpasand Beverages, when its auditor, Deloitte, resigned on 29 May 2018, a few days before its annual results were due. The reason, the auditor said, was that the management wasn't giving them some crucial information required to complete the audit. The stock tanked over 50 per cent in two days, even as management made some excuses, and appointed a different auditor (who also resigned within a year).

Manpasand, before that, was a tale the markets wanted to tell – the maker of an elusive drink called 'Mango-Sip', it was supposed to be the new rage, as long as you could actually find someone who had ever consumed it!

But the analysts seemed to like it, and the large brokers and fund managers even bought into the story. Of course, every portfolio will have a nasty side and some underperformers, but some of the money managers stayed married to Manpasand even after the trouble came to light. The auditors, it turns out, had resigned for good reason – within three years, the company was close to becoming history.

My learning from all this: You should be a little aloof and not get too cosy with management. You needed the numbers to work for you. You needed to learn about the red flags in companies. And you needed to avoid buying if there were red flags.

It was soon starting to become a full-time job. Because it wasn't just about owning great stocks; you had to also find the next great stock, and slowly build positions. It became complicated because I wanted, in my heart, to know so much about a company that I was confident of their success.

But as an entrepreneur, something struck me. I had started two businesses, and run a third. There was a success, a failure, and a so-so kind of result, but if you'd asked me which one would have been a wild success, I think I'd have been more enthusiastic about the ones that didn't succeed. How then could I know enough about a business that I didn't even manage? Was it even possible to know about what's really happening, just by looking at the data from the outside?

How lucky do you have to be to say that's the reason you won?

Value traps

I had this insight that stocks that are somehow worth more than the market is valuing them should be like shooting ducks in a barrel. You can't miss!

Take this example. There is this company named Smartlink. It sold a chunk of its business to Schneider Electric, in 2011. For a sum of Rs 503 crore. And interestingly, the company's market capitalization at the time was Rs 240 crore. Which means: If you bought every share of the company at the current price, you would pay Rs 240 crore. You then own the company, which has cash of Rs 400 crore (after taxes).

Effectively you could pay Rs 80 to own a share, where the company actually has cash of Rs 130 per share.

You're paying 60 paise to own a rupee! Isn't that wonderful?

Before I tell you how that worked out, let me tell you another story. There's a stock named Tata Investments. This is a holding company controlled by you know who. Tata Investments owns a bunch of Tata companies. Like Tata Motors and Tata Steel. But they also own stakes in a substantial number of non-Tata companies. Such as HDFC Bank and Reliance Industries and other big names. In March 2020, if you added up the market value of their holdings in just listed stocks and mutual funds, you would get a whopping Rs 7400 crore or Rs 1576 per share.

But the price in March 2020 was Rs 660 per share. You might say, oh, there was a pandemic. But even a year later, in May 2021, the value of their holdings was Rs 2750 per share and the market price was a mere Rs 1110.

How is this even possible? If I took over the entire company and sold the underlying stocks, I could get more than double my money. Isn't this a bargain?

Sure it is. But Tata Investments has always been a bargain. The stock has traded between 40 per cent and 50 per cent of its 'intrinsic value'. This is what you call a 'value trap'. You can see there's value. It's so obvious because the stuff they own is listed – just take the quantity and multiply by the current market price of each stock, and you get the value of what they own. And yet, no one's willing to pay more than 50 per cent of that value, in the stock market.

There are many such companies. Bajaj Holding, for instance, owns a significant chunk of shares in the Bajaj group of companies. It trades at about 60 per cent below the value of the stocks it owns. Bombay Burmah Trading Corporation (BBTC) has ownership in Wadia companies like Britannia and Bombay Dyeing, and typically trades at 60 per cent discount to the value it holds.

This discount is not without reason. Promoter companies typically don't sell their stocks. They hold because they want to continue to control those companies. If you're a promoter, you don't want to get voted out of key decisions, so you own significant chunks of the stock. These holding companies may be listed, and they are effectively promoters of group companies, but they will not sell the shares they own, because they want to keep control.

You can keep buying the holding companies at a discount to their value, and you won't make any money because the shares will never be sold. (Plus, the holding companies themselves are majority held by the promoters – like Wadias, or Tatas, or Bajaj. So you'll never own enough shares to force them to sell and cash out.)

Given that, promoter holding companies are just value traps. They might never realize the value of the underlying assets. So the market discounts them substantially. Buying them for 'intrinsic value' is a waste of money.

Tata Investments is an even stranger beast, because the Tata companies are only about 60–70 per cent of what they own. The rest of their portfolio is actually unrelated stocks, like HDFC Bank and Infosys and Reliance Industries, which they might have no qualms about selling. (And they do.)

In that situation, the low price of the holding company is even more peculiar. If you just sell the non-Tata stocks in their portfolio, you'll get the market price of the stock! But remember, the market doesn't have to listen to your logic. It has a logic of its own. If it refuses to value Tata Investments as per your logic, you may never realize the profits you calculated so painstakingly.

A value trap is a frustrating way to participate in the market, I realized. You might put a little bit of your money here, but there's no reason why such stocks should be your ticket to a long-term paradise.

The Smartlink story has an interesting follow up. The stock itself didn't do anything. It was at Rs 80 in 2011. It was about Rs 85 in 2021. It continued to remain at about 30 per cent discount to the cash it owned during all of this time.

Yet, the promoter used complicated manoeuvres to pay back cash to shareholders. It's horrendously inefficient to pay dividends in India – before 2020, dividends were not taxed in shareholder hands, so the companies would have to pay 20 per cent before they dished it out. And after 2020, companies didn't have to pay a dividend tax, but shareholders would instead. The dividend is treated as income and is taxed just like interest income is.

The promoter of Smartlink, after paying some dividends, decided to take the 'buyback' route to return cash, buying back 20 per cent to 25 per cent of their stock in total across four different occasions after 2016. This means shareholders sell some of their shares back to the company, receiving cash in exchange. The number of outstanding shares shrinks on the buyback, so the shareholder now has a bigger stake if she doesn't tender her shares.

Effectively, even if the stock price was stagnant, the return on investment, through all the buybacks and dividends, has been a very decent 19 per cent per year. (This is twice what the Nifty has done.) So a value trap might still do well, just not via a stock price increase.

However, there was something else going on, I realized, as I looked at value traps. The market price of a stock is often not going to reflect the fundamentals. But what if the price itself is more important than anything else?

The Gujaratis say 'Bhaav bhagwan che' (The price is God). If you're religious, this means you don't question the price – it's more important than anything else.

If you're not religious, just assume you are, temporarily!

Anyhow, as an investor I had to look at the price thing. Was it useful to be thinking harder about prices?

Prices: 'Trading' and 'technical'

Patterns are interesting. You see a set of numbers like this:

1, 3, 5, 7 . . .

And you might say the next number is 9. There's no reason other than your identifying the pattern looking at the previous data. You 'think' that the pattern sticks on. Unless it's alternate days of the week, in which case the next number is actually 2. But even that is a pattern, once you know.

The point is this – if you see a pattern in the numbers, it's likely that the pattern continues. Stock markets have daily prices. Sometimes those prices form similar patterns. A stock price that keeps going up every week, or every month, might actually see those prices continue upwards. And in reality this almost *always* happens. A stock that's going up, tends to keep going up. And if it falls, it keeps falling for a while.

This is not going to happen forever. The patterns will always break at some point. But if they last enough for you to make a profit, who cares? Do you have to own stocks forever? Can you not exit when the stocks stop going up? And return to them when they restart their upward journey?

There's an entire field of investment involved in trading only by looking at prices. Let the fundamentals folks determine when they want to buy. If there's enough interest in a stock, the prices will go up. If prices go up, there will be a trend. If that trend continues, then buying the stock will result in a profit. This philosophy is called trend-following – and it's one of the ways to play the market using prices alone. How do you analyse if there is a trend? There are statistical methods for looking at prices, and when this is done in financial markets, it's called technical analysis.

You have the standard statistical concepts: Take the moving average of a stock price. This is simply the average of, say, the last ten days of prices. If we're looking today, we sum up the last ten days of prices (not today), and average, just the same way you'd look at Virat Kohli's batting scores. Taken yesterday, it was the ten days before yesterday. The 'window' of ten days moves every day, which is why it's a moving average.

Why ten? It may be 20, 100, 200 – the number of days is something you choose. Now twenty days is typically a month of trades (since markets are closed on weekends) – so a twenty-day moving average (20 DMA) will give you the average of the stock price for the past month.

If a stock trades above its 20 DMA, it's in an uptrend. If it was trading below it, and then moves to above the 20 DMA, it's a 'crossover'. Which could tell you this – if I buy this stock, and this trend sustains, I will make a profit.

But often, something as simple as this is not very tradable. Because a stock could whipsaw – move above one day, and move below the next. So you could add more parameters. A stock needs to be above both the 20 DMA and the 100 DMA. That might tell you a trend. You can even 'back-test' this possibility because you know the past prices. You can say, 'If I'd done this last year, would I have made money?' The answer is easy to calculate – just run it as if it had been done last year, and see the results.

This is useful – 'prices are true'. You can tell me the stock deserves to trade higher, or lower, because of blah-blah-cash-blah-blah-great-future, etc. But that is subjective, and your opinion. Which, pardon my brutal honesty, is worth poppycock in the market. The price is what it is. It's true because someone bought at that price and someone sold. And if the stock is liquid – meaning, enough buyers and sellers – you can also buy or sell at that price.

Technical analysis says this is the only truth that matters – at what price can you buy or sell today?

If prices are true, and they form patterns, can we not profit from the analysis of prices themselves? You don't forecast. You follow. You assume a pattern works, and have a plan for what happens if it doesn't work.

There are many, many ways of trading prices.

Trend-following

As I mentioned earlier, the idea here is to identify a trending pattern, and enter at the early part of a trend, and exit when the trend is over. This is far more difficult than it sounds. Because when stocks go up suddenly, our first reaction is: Oh, this is crazy, the price has to come down. I thought that too. Until I looked a little closer.

I thought, 'Let's see stocks that made new one-year highs'. You could safely assume that a stock that makes a new one-year high is in an uptrend. If I just bought all the stocks that make new one-year highs, and sold them if they ever fell 10 per cent from the highest point after I bought them, I'd be a trend-follower. This simple strategy seems to make a profit, even if you take just the top 50 stocks (the Nifty 50).

There are of course many variations on these methods. Why not wait for a fall of 20 per cent instead? You can test that too. Testing a trend-following framework requires a software program that can take raw data and test your hypothesis, where you can code your strategy.

There are many such programs available – the most popular being amibroker.com and ninjatrader.com. A set of other sites also allow you to 'test' your hypothesis better. This is not a trivial process – you will need to understand statistics, trading techniques and also the art of running the back test. We won't go into this in detail at this point, but suffice it to say that trading with a trend is an established way to make money in the markets.

The biggest problem here is behavioural – you need discipline. It goes so much against our grain to expect trends to sustain that we tend to belittle any opinion that says so. Since we are afraid that the trend will turn the minute after we invest, we think that anyone making money trading a trend is just lucky and undeserving. Nothing could be further from the truth.

In reality, everything you do is lucky and 'undeserving' in that sense. You've won the 'ovarian' lottery, as Warren Buffett eloquently put it, by just being born in an age and geography that allows you to learn some skills and put them to meaningful use. This doesn't mean you aren't actually good at what you do. You have to be both good and lucky. The labourer may be excellent at his task. But he won't get to make anything as much as you will, because hey, ovarian lottery. But we digress.

That trends sustain is a core reality. We have always witnessed it. Sachin Tendulkar, Virat Kohli, Steffi Graf, Serena Williams, Lewis Hamilton, LeBron James. They're all sportspersons. They all have a characteristic pattern of winning continuously sometimes – and we say they are in 'form'. The form is nothing but a trend, and there's no reason that someone else couldn't hit a tennis ball better than Roger Federer – it's just that Federer could do it consistently better than anyone else. If you were to bet on a winner in a match with 'FedEx' at his prime, you'd bet on FedEx. And you accept that, even though once in a while the underdog wins.

You can say a player gets more confident when she wins. Which helps her in her next game, and when she wins that, a little more confidence comes in, and so on. Winning is a game of the mind, in sport, so the benefit perhaps explains a trend. What's the equivalent for companies? The answer: Confidence. Let me explain.

If a company's stock price is going up and making new highs, even the suppliers and customers are probably aware of it. They then find it more comforting to do business with the company compared to, say, if its stock price were plummeting. The additional business effort means better earnings, which then makes the stock price go even higher, and so on. The confidence can also help it raise more capital if it needs to – even the financiers say that if the stock price is going up, we can be less worried the company will not pay back. Confidence can do wonders to humans. It can also do wonders to businesses. Trends just happen.

And thus, following a trend is likely to be profitable. But you are likely to lose a lot of trades when trend-following, so you must ensure that for every time that you lose, you get out early, and when you win, you stay in the trade. If you:
- Win only 50 per cent of the times that you take a position
- Every time you lose, you lose 10 per cent
- But every time you win, you make 20 per cent

Then a Rs 1,00,000 investment, split over, say, ten positions of Rs 10,000 each, will lose on five positions. This is a loss of Rs 5000 since you only lose 10 per cent on each trade.

But the remaining five times, you win. Each win gets you 20 per cent. Since you bet Rs 10,000 each time, you make a profit of Rs 2000 per win, and for five wins, that's a profit of Rs 10,000.

If you win Rs 10,000 and lose Rs 5000 – you still retain a net profit of Rs 5000. Repeat this sort of return over and over, and you actually make serious money over time. You have to, however, stick to the system; most people get so enamoured with the stocks they own that they just don't sell them when they should. This lack of discipline is like Federer occasionally hitting the ball into the net from a lapse of concentration, or Kohli letting one ball slip through between bat and pad. Trading a trend is, therefore, also a mind game as much as anything else.

What if you could try something else? Don't stocks oscillate? They go up as well as down, so is it possible to make money off the fluctuations?

Mean reversion

There's this thought process that if stocks go too far in one direction, they'll come back to the average. Take the 20 DMA we discussed before. Can a stock stay forever above its 20 DMA? Possibly not, because at some point, it's going to take a breather and the moving average, being a little slow, will catch up. And you might be able to take a short-term position on a move that takes it back to the moving average. You can sell at the extreme and buy it back when the stock reverses.

Or take cycles. Every commodity has a cycle. Steel and aluminium do, and so do tyres and petrochemicals and even food items. When the stocks in the sector are in despair, you could check to see if it's at the bottom of a cycle, and take a meaningful bet that the cycle will turn around. Sugar in India is a classic example, because it peaks every few years and then goes back to the bottom soon after.

People in the cycle hate the idea of the cycle turning against them, so they keep saying the four magic words: *This time it's different.* This is usually a defensive statement made in an aggressive tone, as if to say, 'You people are stupid, this time we won't fall like we did last time.' And invariably, in a truly cyclical industry, prices do revert.

A bet on mean reversion would be to buy such sectors when they are in the doldrums, and to exit when everyone tells you that *this time it's different.* The mean reversion tendency is quite likely to ensure that prices come back to more understandable levels over time.

I couldn't really get my head around the mean reversion concept. Even in cycles, I was focused on the trends – uptrends and downtrends, which are part of the cycles. You could trade a trend even as a stock reverted to its mean.

Given that, I won't bother going further into the concept of mean reversion too much. Let's just say that there are people who've made money trading this concept and you could be one of them.

Arbitrage

Someone wants to sell you mangoes at Rs 100 a kilo. But there's people in the apartment complex that will buy those mangoes at Rs 150 a kilo. If you buy at Rs 100 and sell at Rs 150, this is an arbitrage – you buy the same thing at one price and sell it at another.

In the markets you could do a clean arbitrage earlier: Buy on the NSE (one of the stock exchanges) and sell on the BSE (another stock exchange). Same stock, different prices. Now if enough people do this, they will cut the price difference to less than the brokerage payable and this is no longer profitable. Clean arbitrage is now largely done by computers, which pick up a trade in microseconds. So don't even bother to match yourself against them.

In other cases, the arbitrage may not be entirely clean. You may have a situation where one company is merging with another, and both are being traded. Take the case of Tata Steel and Bhushan Steel. After Tata Steel acquired Bhushan in a bankruptcy bid, Bhushan continued to trade in the exchanges. Eventually they decided to merge the two stocks at a ratio of 1 Tata Steel share for every 15 shares of Bhushan.

So if Tata Steel was at Rs 900 per share, then Bhushan Steel should have been at Rs 60 per share, you would think. After all, they've announced the merger ratio, and the merger will happen at some time in the future.

But no, it wasn't. Bhushan Steel would trade at, say, Rs 55. Effectively, you could buy 15 shares of Bhushan Steel, and when the merger happened, you would get a Tata Steel share for Rs 825 (15 x 55) which is much lower than the Rs 900 that Tata Steel was traded at.

This wasn't a clean arbitrage, because there's an element of risk. Tata Steel might change its mind about the merger. Or change the ratio. Or delay the process for years. Or the Tata Steel price might move the wrong way. Even if it works, the time frame is crucial. Getting a 10 per cent differential over a year makes sense, but if this arbitrage takes three years, that's just 3 per cent a year, which isn't so great. This creates room for error, so the arbitrage is 'statistical'.

Special situations

Now many 'special' situations happen in the corporate world. The most common is a merger or demerger. A Swedish company called ABB which had a listed subsidiary in India sold its worldwide power grid operations to Hitachi. In India, they decided not to pursue a slump sale of the power grid business, but instead demerged the Power Grid division of the company from ABB India.

The newly created company ABB PowerIndia was fresh in the market, and very few people knew much about it. At a price of Rs 800 per share, few people could get to the crux of what it really could be worth, except if you looked closely. This was a company providing solutions to the electric vehicle industry. It was a big player in digital power transmissions and so on. The scope of this was quite huge, and it turned out that the stock quickly doubled in less than a year. However, the problem here was just the information dissonance, and if you looked deeply and understood it properly, you might have taken advantage.

While that is qualitative, there are more quantitative situations. Like buybacks. In India there's a rule that if a company buys back its shares in a tender offer, it has to reserve 15 per cent of the issue for people that own shares worth less than Rs 2,00,000. This creates an opportunity. Since typically buybacks are at about 10 per cent higher prices than the market price, could you not buy shares and tender them?

The answer requires a complex set of calculations, involving the following:

- How many shareholders do you estimate, hold less than Rs 2,00,000 worth?
- If they all tender, what's the 'acceptance ratio'? If 200 shares are tendered in the reserved category and the reservation is only for 100, then only half the shares tendered will be accepted.
- What's the risk on those remaining shares, which will come back to you? As an example, if the buyback price is 10 per cent higher and the acceptance ratio is only 50 per cent, that means if you tender 500 shares, 250 are bought back by the company at a 10 per cent higher price. The remaining 250 shares return to you. Now what if the market price falls 15 per cent? You're a net loser.

All this, put into mathematical terms, gives you a probability of investing and making a profit in this special situation: The buyback.

Such special situations can be of benefit to those with a quantitative bent of mind.

By this time, you're probably thoroughly confused. There's the fundamentals and balance sheets and all that. There are value traps. Then there's cyclicals. Then trend following with just price patterns. Or mean reversion, or arbitrage. Or special situations. What do I do?

The answer lies in one thing: Discover who you are.

Discovering who you are

People often find the investing style they like. This means they have to try different styles, and then choose the one that suits them best. People like to follow their heroes, say, Warren Buffett.

But often, they don't have the genetic make-up or the discipline of a Buffett to consistently stick to a process. They'll try a few things and then something else and mix it all together and get entirely lost.

But if you give different styles a try, you might find that one of them works for you. Or perhaps a few of them. The different styles of operation of each of these mechanisms allow you to automatically diversify.

One way I have found easier to work with is price momentum along with fundamentals. You find stocks through the trend-following mechanism. Stocks making new highs, or stocks going up strong. Then a deeper analysis done through a check on the balance sheets, profits and cash flows. Another look at news and management quality. And then you have a set of stocks you might like. When the price momentum is lost, you reduce your position size and wait for the next opportunity to pick up more stocks.

There's no fear of being in cash – when opportunities are few, there's no need to be invested. You can find stocks at leisure, and only participate when they are trending upwards.

You might be a different person. You might love the concept of arbitrage and day trading. Buy stocks and sell them in five minutes. There are people who love this. Others make money through value investing by buying stocks that are severely underpriced, and waiting for years to see them positively rerated. Doing different things takes a little more effort than mastering one thing, but it gives you a lot more perspective.

Looking at markets from different vantage points can be priceless. From a technical charting perspective, from the fundamental analyst perspective, and even from the perspective of a special situations trader. You may have your own style, but the way to look at the market is not just to see how you react to news and changes, but to also estimate how others see the same things.

This is horribly difficult to explain. It's like telling a couple that parenting is insane, nearly suicidal, and yet the most amazingly rewarding thing ever. They will never understand. And yet, most parents, once they're in the process, are naturally inclined to agree. It has to be experienced, because of the complexity of the emotions. And it's different for everyone.

I wouldn't compare investing too closely to child-rearing, because a child is your responsibility whether you like it or not. You can always choose to ignore the concept of investing directly and choose mutual funds instead. The similarity is that the emotional roller coaster of investing has to be lived through to be properly understood.

The most important thing, we realize over time, is the art of money management.

Money management: The idea of a portfolio return

We love to select stocks. Or mutual funds. What can I buy now is often the question, especially every time the markets go up. We love this concept of action all the time. Every day.

Yet, money is made, all too often, by the simple act of just investing regularly with discipline.

Think about this. Say you invest in 10 stocks every month. It's the same stocks, except you replace a few of them every three years. Some stocks will go up. Some stocks will fall. You choose to invest a little more in stocks that have gone up, and a little less in stocks that have fallen. Over the years, this simple concept can make you far more money than any energetic action. You don't need EVERY stock to give you phenomenal returns – just a few will do.

Since you don't know which of these stocks will give you insane returns, you just invest in all, rewarding the ones that do well with a little more money every month.

A stock I liked in 2015 was a little company called Garware Wall-Ropes. They made ropes and fishing nets and sports nets. Synthetic ropes. Boring business? Possibly, but they had very little competition in India. And the business was doing well, reducing debt and increasing profits regularly. The stock was at Rs 200 or so.

Within a couple of years, the stock was at Rs 600. Sounds great? Want to book your profits? Don't, because a year later it was at Rs 1000. In early 2020, it crossed Rs 1500. And in early 2021 it was above 2600 per share.

This isn't to say this trend will last forever. It's had ups and downs. But when you have 10 stocks, if only one of them goes 10x in terms of returns, you want that stock to be the biggest in your portfolio. You don't want to keep booking profits from that stock and putting more money in another stock which is great on paper but is just not moving at all.

The art of money management is to ride your profits and reduce your ownership of the stocks that aren't winning. In this context, you might have to let some stocks become really large chunks of your portfolio. If I'd started with Garware with 10 per cent of my portfolio and nine other similar stocks, then in six years, Garware would have been about 50 per cent of my portfolio if all the others were stagnant.

However, 50 per cent in one stock may not be desirable for diversification, so you can set rules like this:
- Maximum 25 per cent of the portfolio in one stock.

- Every month, when you have money, keep buying the same stocks. Don't keep looking for new ones.
- If a stock does well, reward it by buying more of it.
- Don't be afraid of replacing stocks or even letting them become really small parts of your portfolio. In the end, the losers don't matter. The winners do.
- Don't get married to your stocks. Even the best will falter. Just make sure that you don't hurt too much – another reason why stock-wise portfolio limits make sense.
- Diversify: Don't put too much money into one sector. Use international investing to get access to different types of stocks.
- Don't keep too many positions at less than 1 per cent of your portfolio. If you do that you might not even beat an index fund.
- Have a strategy to enter and exit. Want to enter? Start with a 3 per cent position and keep building up as price rises. Need to exit? Exit half of the position first, and wait a while to exit the rest.
- Know when to break the above rules. There will be enough extreme cases in your lifetime that you'll learn when the rules may not apply and everything has to change. It's usually temporary and you will find yourself getting back to these rules over and over again.

My journey's taken various twists and turns. I'll explain in more detail about an investing process for various types of people. But before that, let's address an important question:

'Deepak, all this is extremely difficult. I just want someone else to take all these decisions for me. How can I do this?'

The answer is: Mutual funds.

What you must watch out for in the stock market

'How do you make an elephant from a slab of rock?'

'You chisel out every part that is not an elephant. What you're left with is . . . an elephant.'

The stock market isn't exactly a place where they invite you in with a smile, offer you the best stocks, and tell you that this one's awesome, and you live happily ever after. This doesn't even happen in the movies nowadays, not even in cartoons.

Don't trust a guaranteed return

Stock markets are risky. They're supposed to be risky. And because they're risky there's a chance of losing money. And then, some people will come and tell you things like:

'Sure shot, guaranteed profit.'

'No risk, just buy, within ten days you'll make money.'

This is attractive, because you want to believe it. Someone you know, or don't know, tells you a sure-shot route to success. And there's no risk. And you get this information for free. It sounds too good to be true and it usually is.

There's a risk in everything, and there's a catch in everything. You need to know what the catch is.

There's an old tale about a scam that originated in physical mail. You would get a letter, saying this: The market will go up this week. Voila, and that week, the market rises. Next week, you get another letter: This week, the market will fall. And it does. Another week, another letter that gets it right. Then they tell you the fourth week's prediction, and a warning: You have to pay a large sum of money to get access to future predictions, otherwise they will stop sending you letters.

They get it right the fourth week too. You pay. The fee is not relevant. This is the holy grail! But strangely, the subsequent weeks their predictions don't work well enough. Sometimes they do, but you lose money trading them. What went wrong?

You were the victim of a scam. What they had was around 8000 addresses. They sent 4000 a message saying the market will go up. The other 4000 were sent a message saying the market will fall.

Based on what the market actually did, there were 4000 messages that were 'right'. To those, the scamsters divided them into 2000 each – and again, one set got the message that the market would go up. The other set, that the market would fall.

You keep chasing the winners, and you have 2000 people in week 2, 1000 in week 3 and 500 in week 4. These 500 have got four consecutive weeks right, and probably love the letters they get. The scamsters now put a large enough fee – Rs 1,00,000 or so, and if 250 of them fall for it, it's Rs 2.5 crore revenue – and after that, they can send paying customers anything they like at random, and that has a 50 per cent chance of working out.

The point is, what seems like the holy grail of investing may just be a massive coincidence, or plain dumb luck, or someone engineering a scheme to sucker you. You should question such things.

We'll see later that NSEL (National Spot Exchange Limited) was party to a scheme where a guarantee was given, of 12 per cent to 18 per cent returns, almost risk-free. When the low-risk opportunities are only 7 per cent elsewhere, like bank fixed deposits, why would someone offer 12 per cent risk-free returns? The scam told us the story – it was a massive Ponzi scheme, where certain borrowers offered those returns by simply borrowing from new suckers who put in their money. Eventually it blew up.

Oh, there are risk free, but low returns. Like arbitrage funds in equity markets. These make money in equity, buying stocks and selling 'futures' (derivatives contract that allows you to decide at what price you want to sell something a month or so later). The difference is a return that's low risk, but the return is also low.

High returns with low risk? Now that's the stuff of legends. You will find them say this. I know for sure that company ABC will go up. Look, I told you that XYZ would go up and it did, no? This is your ticket to freedom. Watch out, because all it will free you from is your money.

Sniff out planted news

In the stock market, you should just be cynical about what you hear. Nearly every single piece of news is manipulated to make it sound the way it does, and thus, drive you to purchase (or sell) a stock. There are people who make a lot of money planting news. It's done nicely and neatly.

They'll say, 'Oh, we want to sell non-core assets.' This should trigger a warning bell. Why would you say you 'want' to sell something, and call it 'non-core', meaning they don't really care about it. The minute you say this in public, everyone who might be a buyer realizes that you really want to get rid of it, and will low-ball you on the price.

Case in point: In an interview, the banker of a wind energy company, Suzlon, said that the company is looking for a buyer for it's 'non-core' assets. This struck me as a problem, for the reason above, but also because this banker was supposed to maximize the value of any such sale. Usually, people will sell and then tell you they sold something and that it was non-core. That way, the deal's already done.

Also note that when a company immediately denies a rumour that has just started bouncing around in the market, you should consider it planted. A news channel will say 'our sources tell us that Company B may be looking to buy company C'. Both stock prices go up, and Company B vehemently denies any idea of the news, and some operators make money. This happens so often that no one seems to care.

Listen to what they do, not what they say

Warren Buffett and his partner Charlie Munger, who took Berkshire Hathaway from a tiny company to an insurance giant, are the go-to guys for everything in finance. Their pithy but hard-hitting one-liners are quoted often, but largely out of context.

'My favourite holding period is forever' is an often-quoted Buffett quote. This is the excuse that people use to hold stocks even after horrible news comes in and wreaks havoc on the stock price. Gotta hold this forever! Except Buffett himself hasn't held things forever. A report by John Hughes, Jing Liu and Meeshan Zhang discovered that Buffett's median holding period of a stock was one year, with 30 per cent of his stocks sold in six months.

Diversification is for the ignorant, goes another 'Buffetism'. Know your stocks enough to concentrate your holdings. Yet, in the 1980s, Berkshire had 95 stocks at one time – and he wasn't as rich as he is today.

Derivatives are weapons of mass destruction, the followers quote. But Buffett is in an industry that uses derivatives often (reinsurance) and he has himself participated in longer term derivative bets.

If the idea is:
- Stick to the rules
- Know when to break the rules

Then it makes sense but if you violate the rules often, you're unlikely to see your 'rules' taken seriously. Warren Buffett is an exceptional investor, but beware of taking his words too seriously. What he does is far more important.

This is true of everything. When people tell you one thing, but they're apparently doing something else, you should be on the side of looking at what they're doing, not what they're saying. People say a lot of things needlessly, and sometimes just to get the questioner off their back. People also change their views with time, and in markets such changes are much required. You might be wrong, but it's criminal to stay wrong.

Which is why taking people too seriously in the markets for their 'strong' opinions is only for the uninitiated. Once you've been bruised and battered, you start believing actions more than words.

A rose by any other name . . . would be bitcoin

There are companies whose names indicate something that's not related to the business. An oxygen shortage during the Covid pandemic led to a spike in the prices of Bombay Oxygen, a listed company. Unfortunately, it had stopped the oxygen business years back and was now a lending finance company. So much for efficient markets.

There's many more instances one can cite of this sort of naming confusion. Talwalkars, a famous gym company that also made lifestyle supplements, once split its business into two different listed companies, called Talwalkar's Lifestyle and Talwalkar's Fitness. But sadly for shareholders, they put the gym business into the company named Lifestyle, and the lifestyle products into the company named Fitness. This confused everyone, with good reason. And the share price of both companies took a hammering eventually.

The name may not indicate what a company does. There's no reason for it to do so. Most of the times you have to look deeper. For the longest time, Tata Salt – a consumer product – was sold by a company named Tata Chemicals – whose primary business is industrial chemicals. There's a product called PediaSure – a baby food product, made by Abbott. But it's not the listed Abbott in India, it's sold by a company privately owned by Abbott, USA. You often need to look a little deeper.

Do not underestimate the value of luck

People think luck is 'unearned' in a derogatory sort of way. Get an out-of-turn promotion because your boss just resigned, and your peers say you got lucky. Someone buys out your company, it's your lucky day.

Yet, luck isn't a bad thing. And sometimes it's the only thing you can bank on. Let me explain.

You buy 20 stocks. They're all good stocks, but none of them is moving the needle for you. Yet, the smallest of the stocks starts to move up, while everything else is down. You have no idea why. It's not in the papers, in the news, or anything else – yet, the stock seems to be moving up. All your 'better' stocks are sitting right there.

You find that the black-sheep stock suddenly reveals a big deal, they get a large deal from an international player and the revenue will triple in two years. You don't know if the market knew it, but there were people who probably did, what with lawyers on each side, and many consultants. Someone bought and took the price up, and you, having been already invested, also received the benefit without realizing why.

Isn't this unearned luck too? You had some conviction in the stock but not enough. You were maybe even close to giving up and selling when suddenly it started to move up. But the point is actually simpler: You were stupid to ever think that your 20 stocks would all do well, and the stock in which you placed the largest conviction will do the best. Leave that story for the TV interviews, because it makes a good story.

The reality is, you have no idea how the market will like your stock. It may own a goose that lays golden eggs and yet, the stock price doesn't go up. The fact that you chose a stock after a lot of work, or that the business itself has performed, means nothing. It takes a bit of luck for the market to discover it too. For many years, sometimes even a decade, a great stock might have languished, testing your patience. You need that little bit of luck; otherwise it doesn't work.

To maximize the impact of luck, you're going to have to diversify and take on multiple bets. That way, if luck shines on a few, that's enough to give you great returns. In fact, you have to work really hard to be able to get lucky.

When opportunity knocks, you gotta open the darn door, not just sit around! So yeah, the people who work hard succeed because they take the luck when it comes and make it work for them. That is not unimportant. Don't take away the wrong meaning that if it's all going to be about luck anyway, let me sit and do yoga while I wait for luck to drop money into my bank account.

But don't attribute your success to skill. You are incredibly lucky if you're part of the top 5 per cent of India, the people who get to invest in stocks. You're incredibly lucky to have lived through an era when the world's central banks ensured you could buy stocks and not lose money. And when you do make money, it's probably due to a lot of the factors you don't control, which work in your favour anyhow and make your success happen.

New Issues

There are companies trying to raise capital all the time. There may be several new issues – IPOs on a given day. Your friendly neighbourhood broker will recommend some of these enthusiastically because they could be getting a fee. Be very reluctant to subscribe to a new issue. We'll explain why in a later chapter. For now, let's just say an IPO is a little like a lottery: You could win big and you could lose big.

Don't catch a falling knife

This is good advice in real life. If you catch a falling knife, you might catch the blade instead and injure yourself instead of letting the knife fall harmlessly to the ground. In the stock market, you will get this advice from people who have had bandaged hands.

Everyone wants to 'average down' – buy much more of a stock when it falls. This works every once in a while, such as just after the stock market tanked during the early days of the Covid-19 pandemic, when stocks fell 40 per cent, but in the next year doubled from their lows. Buying those lows would have given you a thrill – what an incredible stock picker you are!

Yet, in most cases, the knives just keep falling. A stock that falls 90 per cent is one that first fell 80 per cent and then halved. Some of these are dud businesses, some see frauds, and others are just going through very tough times. One example: Dewan Housing Finance Limited (DHFL).

In the middle of 2018, something strange happened. DHFL's stock was falling heavily. The stock market as a whole wasn't doing that badly, but the DHFL stock price was down 40 per cent in a single day. From Rs 616, the stock collapsed to Rs 347 in an eventful but confusing trading session – no one knew why this non-banking home lender, which had given over Rs 1,00,000 crore in loans, was falling heavily. But to the knife catcher, this sounded juicy, as an opportunity that appears once in a lifetime. In fact, DHFL was at the 360 levels in 2017, before it nearly doubled. Was it time to catch the falling knife hoping to hold the handle?

By the end of the year 2018, the DHFL stock was at Rs 250, another 30 per cent down. Wasn't this the opportunity you had been waiting for? Within two more months, in February 2019, the stock fell below Rs 100. That's a 60 per cent drop from the Rs 250 that it was a bargain the second time around.

The company eventually struggled through bankruptcy and in May 2021 the stock languished at Rs 18. The knives have bled a lot of people out. If you really like a company, perhaps it's best to wait till the stock price recovers a good portion of those losses before you get back in. The best time to catch a falling knife is never.

Bankrupt is not your friend

In India, there's a weird history to bankruptcy. Companies go bankrupt all the time. Their business takes a downturn; they lose money; they can't repay their loans; and then it's time for the next step: They ask the lender (or lenders) for a 'restructure'.

The conversation with the banks goes something like this:

'You owe us fifty crore rupees.'

'I don't have it.'

'Okay, how much can you repay?'

'Twenty crore, but you must let me pay it back over five years.'

'Fine, let's cut the base down to twenty crore and then start over. We, the banks, will take the loss of thirty crore rupees.'

This is clearly an insane thing to do. Why? Because banks should have asked for equity shares instead, worth the Rs 30 crore they write off. So that when the business revives, the banks can participate in the recovery and make back some of that money later by selling the shares in the market.

But that was impossible, because RBI rules didn't allow banks to own more than 10 per cent of any listed stock. In many such cases, the dilution would have led to the bank owning 50 per cent or more. And there were takeover rules.

If you took over 26 per cent stake in a stock you had to make other shareholders an 'open offer' to buy their shares up to another 26 per cent stake. Why would any lender agree to this? So the banks had to just swallow the losses. Better to lose 30 crore than 50 – that was the thought process.

Due to these weird and complicated rules, the promoters had a field day. They'd slowly siphon out money from the borrowed loans, into their own pockets. Then they would go ask for a restructure. The banks would agree. The promoters could now keep the money without the need to pay it back.

Shareholders also found this interesting. It was a 'special situation'. When the company started discussions for restructuring, people started to buy the stock in the market.

They thought, the banks will write off loans, which makes the company healthier. But banks also can't take equity stake, which would have diluted the value of our stake. So it's win-win for the shareholder.

> *Note:* In order for a bank or anybody else to take a fresh stake, the company would have to issue fresh shares to the bank in lieu of the cash it couldn't pay. As the paid-up capital increased, the stakes of other shareholders would become less. Like, if there are 100 shares in the company and the bank is issued a fresh 100 shares, everybody else's ownership is halved in terms of percentage of ownership.

The bankruptcy code (IBC 2016) came along in 2016, and the RBI changed the rules. Banks could now own more than 10 per cent of a company. Banks would also not qualify as promoters, and would not need to make open offers.

When you put a company through bankruptcy, you look for a 'resolution' – and a part of that resolution is to enable all lenders to take large equity stakes in the bankrupt business. Sometimes this resolution process results in such large dilution that existing shareholders go from owning 100 per cent of the company (pre-bankruptcy) to 3 per cent after the bankruptcy is done. This happened in Monnet Ispat where the acquirer (JSW Steel) got 75 per cent of the company (with new shares issued), lenders got another 19 per cent, and the remaining shareholders were left with only 6 per cent put together.

In other cases, like in Lakshmi Vilas Bank (LVB), which went through a quick resolution in 2020, all the existing shares were written down to zero. The acquirer, DBS Bank, got 100 per cent ownership of the bank. If you owned a share in LVB, you got zero for it after the resolution.

This means that the earlier bet of 'oh, I should buy this bankrupt company's shares, they might revive it' is now just wrong. There's no reason why you will benefit any more – the company can simply write off all its shares. You have to remember this: This is the essence of capitalism. Companies die, and when they do, shareholders bear the losses.

Think of a portfolio, not a stock

A friend comes up to you and says, 'Look, I bought this Yes Bank share, and it's up 30 per cent.' You admire him for it. And ask him, 'How much did you put in it?'

'Ten thousand rupees,' he says.

You know he is worth over Rs 50 lakh. So 30 per cent on Rs 10,000 is like peanuts. Why would he care? The answer is peculiar: Because it makes him feel good.

A stock up 30 per cent indicates skill. The skill doesn't have to translate to high profit in absolute terms. The best mechanic in the world may not be able to earn as much as a mediocre manager – the fact that you have some skill doesn't mean you can earn a great deal from it.

People want to show off their skills. They don't necessarily want to convert that to the ability to make great money. The discovery of this behavioural trait can be painful. In this case, you tell your friend: 'Dude, all that is great but just three thousand rupees is ridiculously little.'

Your friend mentally says, *'He's right. If I knew about Yes Bank I should have put more money. In fact, I should have put most of my money on it.'*

The next opportunity he sees, he puts up a huge amount of money. And that company goes bust. Because that's how things sometimes pan out. And your friend loses money. So the next time you meet him, you ask:

'What are you buying now?'

'The stock market is rigged,' he says. 'Full of manipulators. I just gave up.'

And you realize what's happened – he wanted to make the returns real, and couldn't deal with the losses, so he walked away. The derision is just him licking his wounds.

The point isn't that he should have bet everything on Yes Bank. Or that he shouldn't have bet the second time. The point is that a portfolio-based approach – where you have many positions – works better than betting on a single stock. In any portfolio – just about any portfolio – you will have stocks that do well, and stocks that are laggards. Most of the portfolio returns will come from one-fifth of your stocks – the rest will remain a blot.

This is why you should care only about how much money you make overall, across the portfolio, rather than individual stocks. Sure, put some effort into understanding the stocks you buy. But also put some effort into diversifying enough that you don't depend too much on a single position. And always look at the overall returns.

Think of this this way. Say you take bets such that when you're up, you double your money. When you're down you lose 50 per cent.

If you bet that way in one single stock, after ten trades, you have five wins and five losses, and you end up at exactly the same amount as when you started! Rs 100 became Rs 50. Then went back to Rs 100. Then down to 50, and back to 100. And so on. Till you're left with just Rs 100. No return. Just the capital.

What if you take two bets of Rs 50 each on two stocks? You lose Rs 25 in one stock (50 per cent) and make Rs 50 on the other stock (100 per cent). You're now up from Rs 100 to Rs 125. If you continue to put half in one stock and half in another, you end up with a far greater return than 0 per cent.

Say you make ten trades on this 'double if I win and half if I lose' principle, on a two-stock portfolio. You have five wins and five losses. But this time your portfolio is up to Rs 305 after ten trades! A 200 per cent return versus 0 per cent if you just put all the money in one stock.

It pays to diversify. And it pays to look at overall portfolio returns. The individual stock returns are not useful to concentrate on. They are only good conversation topics at parties.

SUCKERED

Sundry scams and sharp practices

Don't get suckered

Stories. Every scam is about telling a story and getting some sucker to believe it. I lived in a hostel during my engineering college days. Those four years were full of such stories – we made up quite a few.

There was the time we wanted our exams postponed. There was a plague outbreak in Surat, which was a few thousand kilometres north of campus. So someone conveniently found a dead rat and raised a fuss; it didn't end well after the authorities, not taken in as we hoped, found evidence that the rat hadn't died of the plague.

We couldn't sucker the profs that time, but that didn't stop us from trying again. We'd go to the doc on campus, and try to get letters to avoid having to go to class. Only, the doc had seen it all before and he would recommend a paracetamol tablet each time, unless you were visibly dying, which was not very often.

Once (this is way before cell phones) we decided to move all the clocks in our wing forward four hours because my roommate wanted to be at the college beach temple (we had a beach, really) at 6 a.m. We might have made it work, except that the sun refused to cooperate by rising early.

When I emerged into the real world, I realized something. People often try to sucker you, but unlike our college escapades, it's not just for the lulz. It's mostly to try to part you from your money.

It's not only the widow from Nigeria who wants you to believe she will give you a hundred million dollars that her late husband stashed away. Those scams are mostly obvious, but there are less obvious ones. These are often disguised as insurance policies.

So let me relate a few stories of financial scams and the suckers who fell for them, and this might help you pretend you're never ever going to be the victim of such a story.

You've been on the other side of these conversations, at some point.

'There's no risk sir, it's guaranteed.'

'See, all the smart people have already bought it, I've sold seven this week, only three are left.'

'It's just like a fixed deposit, ma'am.'

'I have inside news that this company is going to announce something big. I'm telling you this, for free, though I'm only your stockbroker.'

You've heard all this, and you've realized after a few years that maybe this whole finance thing is a scam. It's not, but who's to know whom to trust when everyone wears a suit?

The problem isn't that you got suckered, or maybe you didn't. The problem is this erodes trust because every scam starts with building trust and making you believe something. You have to trust someone, but the problem is that you can't blindly do so.

This chapter is about many of the things that have suckered people in the past. It's organized, more or less in order of suckerage, if there is such a word. (There isn't, trust me, because I just made it up.)

Suckered

Some of this is the stuff of legends – the outright scams. The illegal kind. Give us your money and we'll give you great returns. Until we don't, ala Ponzi. The jeweller and his uncle that stole billions from a bank. The company that said it made money, but lied.

Then there are the traps. This is like when you order this awesome huge bunch of apples online, to get wax miniatures.* It's not necessarily illegal ('It was a zoomed image') but it's definitely immoral.

Indians love to create complicated rules and then work out the loopholes. We adore loopholes. We even have religious tales to this effect. So let me segue into a religious story and then, when you're wondering what this is all about, I'll revert to the topic of discussion with a profound observation of how this applies to the financial world.

There was this demon called Hiranyakashipu. This is ridiculously tough to spell, or pronounce, so we'll just call him H. Now H had a serious problem with Vishnu, who's a god and therefore not easy to mess with. But H worked out a divide-and-conquer strategy and prayed hard to Brahma, another seriously powerful god.

Brahma offered him a boon.

H said, 'I shouldn't die inside or outside my house. I shouldn't die in the day or in the night, in the ground, or in the sky. Not by a weapon, not by a human, or an animal.'

Brahma said fine, because no one reads the fine print anyhow.

H then started doing nasty things to people who liked Vishnu, who, I repeat, was not someone you mess with. So Vishnu took the form of 'Narasimha' – half man, half lion – and

---

*Wax miniatures of food should be illegal, but we digress.

emerged from the wall of H's palace. He killed H at twilight (neither day nor night), on the threshold of his house (neither inside, nor outside), using his lion's claws (not a weapon) while suspending H off the ground across Narasimha's thigh (so not on the ground, or in the sky).

The point: Brahma's boon and H's conditions for immortality had loopholes. Vishnu figured out those loopholes. He didn't just use divinity to override the boon – that would be the divine equivalent of illegal and, quite possibly, have led to bad blood between him and another god. H was suckered, because he didn't read the fine print.

Nowadays, in the financial industry we call this 'Terms & Conditions apply'.

We love our loopholes and in times of good versus evil, we admire the good person who overcomes evil by finding a loophole. But most of the time, it's the evil people who think these up, and use them to sucker the good.

There's such a strong cultural tradition of looking for, and using, embedded loopholes in India that it's not even considered wrong, especially in the financial world. 'There's a sucker born every minute, and he's going to help me make my monthly quota' is the financial service provider's mantra. Indeed, most of us would agree there's nothing wrong with people trying to exploit loopholes, so long as the money doesn't evaporate from your pocket.

Scams fall into patterns. If you know the stories and the stuff that's been thrown at us in the past, your antenna might go up in the future. We'll try to tell some of those stories and educate you, in a simple, direct, entertaining way with few long words and sentences.

So read on and you'll learn how we've been suckered, and paid our dues in various ways.

Five easy ways to get suckered

It used to be fashionable for men to show their scars, to show they'd suffered more than the other guy. In the same spirit, let's discuss how one gets suckered into buying various things. Here are five common ways in which people regularly get conned.

Asking your banker where to invest

This is like asking a barber if you need a haircut. In fact, if you asked your banker if you needed a haircut he would likely say yes, and then try to work out a deal where he recommends a barber who pays him 6 per cent commission.

Legends say that once upon a time bankers were staid, honest, hard-working people who would know who you were, remember your birthday, and advise you not to buy that car because you couldn't afford it. That breed either never existed, or it has retired, or maybe been kicked upstairs into management.

The banker you'll meet is a 'customer-facing relationship manager' who sees you as a target parked at a centre of a pattern of alternating black and white concentric circles. In fact, they even call you a 'target' when they're talking shop among themselves.

One of the best ways to get conned is to ask for a 'safe' investment avenue with 'maximum returns'. This is the point in a movie when the subtitle flashes 'Sucker' in italics. With a broad smile, the relationship manager will immediately whip out a product where, after complex calculations, you get 25 per cent of your investment.

You might feel happy until you read that sentence again, and you find that all you will get is 25 per cent of your investment. That is, 75 per cent will disappear.

In many cases, you will only get to know years later that you lost an entire year's worth of monthly 'investment' cheques, as commission paid to the 'relationship manager', who has now found gainful employment elsewhere.

Nowadays, commissions are so complexly intertwined in financial products that, after initial outrage, you admire the guys who thought up these structures and these campaigns. They use advertisements which show your children becoming the rock stars you always wanted to be. This is just to make you believe an insurance product (of all things) will make your children rock stars.

The only problem is that by the time the kids are ready to become rock stars, the cost of the guitar has far surpassed whatever crumbs are left to you after all the commissions have been paid. And to top it, your kids probably listen to absolutely horrendous music.

Versions of this story can be served up as sides when you're sitting around with friends and downing gallons of beer. That's one thing these scams are good for. The beer consumption at least will help to grow GDP.

Going with the 'heard' mentality

I have this friend who seems to have made a lot of money investing in stocks. He keeps telling me the names of stocks that he bought and how he made a ton of money. Like he bought Satyam at Rs 20 in 2008 (it has now merged with Tech Mahindra and as of 2021 given the equivalent of a 12x return from the Rs 20). And he also bought Infosys at Rs 100 in 1994 (Infosys is trading at Rs 1325 after multiple stock splits and bonuses and a Rs 100 investment in 1994 is now Rs 2,25,000 in market value). And he bought Unitech at . . . okay, he never even bought Unitech. (Furiously erases lines from demat statement, because Unitech trades in 2021 at Rs 2.60 and it was once Rs 500.)

Well, it seems everything he bought turned to gold, so I should listen to him. He subscribes to a tip service that only charges if you make profits. And these tips tell you to buy 50 stocks every day. Some of this laundry list will definitely make a profit, so they can bill him for as long as they want.

Some of the ideas are seductive but crazy. In 2011 a company named Atlas Copco delisted (the shares were bought back by the promoters who then pulled the company off the stock exchange) at a price much higher than expected, netting 50 per cent profit for lucky shareholders within a month.

My friend's tipsters have now compiled a list of all such companies that have a microscopic chance of getting delisted, and they're telling everyone to buy these. That plan goes something like this. I'll buy first. Then, other investors will buy and the price will go up and these stocks will be delisted at even higher prices. Never mind that many of these promoters won't buy back at the current price, leave alone paying a premium if the stock price rises.

People who listen to tipsters often say, 'Tell me, if I don't listen to other people, how will I know where to invest?' Well, let's say my friend told me the best-ever car was the Maruti Versa. And Amitabh Bachchan advertised it, so it must be the best car around . . . Would you buy this car without a test drive, or even if you read on the internet that they were going to discontinue manufacture?

Listen to people by all means, but don't suspend your judgement or blindly take advice.

The great initial public offer

The heard mentality also goes nuts about IPOs. Every new company going public is a multi-bagger if you listen to the khabar.

'The latest IPO is linked to the <insert name of famous political family> and it will only go up. Look at the demand! Look at the Coal India IPO – it went up 30 per cent!'

But they don't tell you to look at the NHPC IPO which had gone down 33 per cent even when the market was up in the interim. They conveniently ignore all the random IPOs that have failed.

IPOs are big money-spinners for the people selling them regardless of the returns the investors get. Oversubscription makes every lead manager happy and it sends the TV channels into a frenzy. So IPOs are sold by any and every means possible.

The most infamous precursor to the Great Indian Crash was the Reliance Power IPO of 2008. The brokers used the Ambani surname like toothpaste and convinced trainloads of investors to borrow money to subscribe to India's largest IPO (at the time) at a whopping Rs 450 per share. The stock price dropped 50 per cent a few days after it listed.

Thirteen years later, after a consolatory bonus issue to irate investors, and a merger with RNRL, the stock price is at Rs 10, in 2021.

IPOs sell well because we like the idea of something new. Remember in our earlier chapter on stocks, we didn't add a section on how to buy IPOs? That wasn't by accident. It needs considerably deeper skills to interpret and analyse IPOs, since the company has little history to go by. The bankers who say it's great also earn a commission from selling the shares, so they're biased.

Buying an IPO for 'listing gains' is a fad that never dies, but it's fraught with risk. When the experienced investor finds reading an IPO prospectus daunting, it's difficult for the novice to find enough meaning to invest with any confidence.

But IPOs are hyped up, and oversubscribed many times over, so much that there is a random lottery conducted to allocate shares. An old hand said this best: If you want an IPO, you're not going to get any shares allocated. If you get any shares allocated, you probably don't want any!

And if you really want to get conned, a great way is to borrow money to buy into the next great IPO. You might make money, or not. Either way, you'll have a tale to tell.

Forgetting the invisible

I can buy a twenty-five-year time share holiday package – one week a year, at any one of forty-odd resorts, by paying a few lakh today and a few thousands every year for maintenance. What I don't see is that I get tied to their properties. If all my favourite places are booked for the Dussehra holidays, as they will be because everyone and their nephew have holidays, I'm out of luck.

I now have to choose between spending more money on a holiday I really want, or go to a place I don't want to be, just to 'recover' my investment (Himalayas in December!).

In a similar spirit, I'll buy a sugar stock on the news that sugar prices have gone up. But I'll forget that in the past, for centuries, the industry has gone through cycles and that higher prices means more sugar will be produced and there'll be oversupply next year. Then the prices will crash.

You'll fall for this sort of scam if you forget the invisible, the unknown, and the past. After all, the ignorant are ignorant of their ignorance. And the education, although expensive, makes for a great story.

I have just won an award of US$1 million from Microsoft.

(That is how the mail goes.) To get that million, all I have to do is give my name, address, PAN, Aadhaar, passport copy, copy of bank account and a small 'fee' for the actual transfer which is stuck in the customs department in Uganda. And then, a little more as a bribe to that Uganda official who needs to sign on the form. Oh, so they need a little more to clear up all pending issues, and perhaps if I could come down to, say, Nigeria, I might be able to meet with the local representative of Microsoft to clear up the matter.

Even if you discount the travel part of it, it's incredible how many people fall for this kind of con job. And because it's so famous, and they can't admit they were conned, it's all under wraps.

The insurance trap

'I'll give you this new plan, sir. You pay one lakh rupees a year for ten years.'

You wonder where this is going, but he's calling you 'sir', so he might have something.

'Then we pay you back eighty-four thousand rupees a year for another ten years.'

Mentally, you're thinking: *Okay I've just got about Rs 16,000 a year invested, so I should now have about 1,60,000 still invested in there.*

'After that, we will give you a lump sum amount of ten lakh rupees.'

In your head, you can hear the 'eureka' happen: 1.7 lakh invested. I get back Rs 10 lakh. That's awesome, you think. 'Where should I sign?' you ask.

'Oh, we also give you insurance of twenty-five lakh rupees so that if you die your wife gets the amount you paid, plus twenty-five lakh rupees back, sir!' says the agent, emphasizing the 'sir' even more. You're almost convinced, and you call your wife.

'Ritu, this is like super awesome!' and you repeat the information on the phone.

'Ajit, have you done the calculations?' says Ritu, and you sense a little bit of cynicism in her voice. The agent is trying to fill in your pan number, so you murmur it to him and tell her confidently, 'Look, after the first ten years they start giving us back the money so technically at the end of twenty years, we only have 1.6 lakh rupees invested, and they'll give us ten lakh rupees. That's like at least 15 per cent or something.'

'But wait, what if I put this in a spreadsheet and calculate what it really means . . .'

'Ritu, I know this stuff, it's foolproof,' you say, smugly waiting because the calculations should prove you right.

'It's 4.8 per cent a year,' says Ritu, and the voice almost hopes she's wrong.

'What, no chance!' you say. She sends you the spreadsheet by mail. It's correct. It's just 4.8 per cent. Less than 5 per cent a year, when a fixed deposit will give you a good 7 per cent.

You do the calculations yet again.

Rs 1 lakh a year for ten years.

At 7 per cent a year, that will grow to Rs 14.8 lakh.

Grow that for another ten years, at 7 per cent, but take out Rs 84,000 every year.

You're left with Rs 16.7 lakh.

Incredible. The insurance company wants to give you back Rs 10 lakh at the end of twenty years. In a fixed deposit, the same thing earns Rs 16.7 lakh – 67 per cent more!

And you were actually excited about it all. You're now angry and you show the agent the calculation.

'Sir, but we also give you the insurance!' the agent says, angrily. It's the best-selling product of the month, and this stupid customer is showing him a spreadsheet?

You look it up, and a simple regular insurance for Rs 25 lakh at the same insurer costs Rs 6000 a year. Take the same insurance separately, and the spreadsheet shows the new number: At the end of twenty years, you have Rs 14 lakh left. By just using a fixed deposit and a separate insurance plan, you make 40 per cent more!

The agent is not going to defend this. 'Why would I give you a bad product, sir? More than thirty people have signed up,' he says frustrated. He makes a mental note never to contact you again. Spreadsheet-walas. They destroy GDP.

You make a mental note to buy a bottle of wine, because Ritu's going to rub it in that you have an MBA, and all she did was take an online course on XIRR.

This sounds like a lot of numbers. But it's simply a product that tells you this: Give me money for ten years. I will give you less than the returns of a fixed deposit.

This sounds extreme. Immediately the family LIC (Life Insurance Corporation) person will jump up and say: *But you also get insurance! It's tax-free! This Deepak Shenoy knows nothing.*

But the key factor here is that Deepak Shenoy knows that he knows nothing.

In this matter, though, let's cut through the BS. There are simpler, very tax efficient products, which will give you at least 40 per cent better returns. But you won't be told about them. Effectively, you're suckered.

Why do you get such lousy returns? It's because of one thing: Commissions. A typical insurance plan pays between 2 per cent and 50 per cent as commissions, and in some extreme cases they will even pay 100 per cent commission!

The big game of insurance

The idea of insurance is simply to say this:

> *If something bad happens to you, we'll pay you some money so that you can tide over the financial pressure that you will incur in those bad times.*

For health insurance, it's like saying if you need to be in a hospital, the bills can be onerous, so insurance can take some (or all) of the hit. For car insurance, an accident can lead to huge repair bills, which the insurance company will pay for.

For this, the insurance company takes a 'premium'. The idea is that if enough people pay their premiums, and only a fraction of them get ill, or have an accident, the insurance company can easily pay up and still profit.

If of course, nothing happens, you don't get back anything. That way, the cost is very, very low, and keeps you covered for an unlikely event.

Life insurance is a different thing. The idea is this:
- Oh, you'll die some day
- So your family needs money to survive going forward
- Buy life insurance – this way, they're covered

How can this be bad? It isn't. This is the simplest form of insurance – called 'term' insurance. The idea is simple: You pay a premium every year, to be covered for a certain term – ten years, or twenty years, or whatever. And then, if you don't die, which is admittedly a good thing, you don't get back any of your money. It's a bet you want to lose.

How much insurance do you need? A rough estimate is that whatever money you have should cover your family expenses for at least the next thirty to forty years. For a thirty-five-year-old, this is roughly about thirty times her family expenses every year – or about 360 times the monthly expense. That means, for a person spending Rs 1,00,000 a month, your need for insurance is roughly Rs 3.6 crore a year.

For a healthy thirty-five-year-old, a term insurance of this kind will only cost Rs 3500 a month or less. Of course if you have enough savings already, you can subtract that from the 360 months of coverage needed, and insure for a lower amount.

This is the good part.

This is also what no one will sell you.

Because there are ways to sucker you into paying more commissions, so agents will always avoid selling you the cheapest option.

'Getting your money back'

Some of you are thinking: I will pay all this money and not get any money back if I survive! Is that the reward for just surviving? Come on.

This is where the pitch starts. Oh, we can offer you an awesome insurance plan. If you survive, you will get your money back, with a bonus!

But there's a catch, a very simple one. You're going to pay more than double the premium you would otherwise pay in a 'term' plan.

Now I could tell you this: Pay me Rs 1,00,000 a year. And I'll give you that insurance cover of Rs 3.6 crore for twenty-five years.

And if you do survive, I'll pay you back all the money you've paid – which is about Rs 25 lakh. Are you okay with this?

This sounds good but I can see your mind already start to get sceptical. Because it's going like this:

If I buy just 'term', I'll pay Rs 40,000 a year

This 'money back' policy asks for Rs 1,00,000 a year

The guy selling the policy could just take the excess Rs 60,000 a year and put it in a bank account

Even at a minimal 5 per cent a year, that money will grow to Rs 28.5 lakh – easily enough to get back all the money paid so far and generate a decent Rs 3.5 lakh in profit.

And here's what I haven't told you: You can do this yourself. Just buy the term plan. Invest the rest. You'll do better.

Don't mix insurance and investment

The three reasons people buy insurance is:
1. To save tax.
2. As an investment, to make a good return on their money.
3. To feel good that one has some insurance, or to get rid of that pesky uncle who keeps mentioning it.

The fourth – and perhaps most important – reason to buy insurance is to let your family be financially secure if you die.

This is the term plan, and it is the only reason anything should be insured.

Car insurance gives you money if your car has an accident, and covers costs for people you might injure. Home fire insurance covers the damages in case there's a fire. You pay every year, and you're happy to not have to claim (because it means you've not had an accident or a fire!); and at the end, you don't get your money back.

Not so with life insurance. Most of the life policies bought are for the purpose of saving or investing, not for insurance. And that is because life insurance is hardly ever bought, it's sold.

The sellers get a fatter commission when they sell you a 'saving' product, so you don't ever get to see the real insurance. 'Pure term' insurance is the only real deal: Your family gets paid if you die, and your premium is lost when you don't. Anything else, usually called ULIPs, money-back, endowment or savings policies, involves a small amount of insurance and a higher degree of saving.

Even if it sounds like killing two birds with one cheque, you shouldn't mix investment and insurance – because you don't get enough of either when you do.

Take a thirty-five-year-old with a monthly salary of Rs 50,000 and expenses of, say, Rs 30,000. The minimum insurance expected would be about Rs 1 crore; the idea is that you need your family to live another forty years off the money, at a current return of around 8 per cent risk-free and expenses rising at an inflation of 6 per cent.

The cost of a 'term' policy of Rs 1 crore could be between Rs 15,000 and Rs 30,000 a year – or Rs 1500 to Rs 2500 a month, easily affordable. But agents find such policies unlikely to give them enough commissions, and they know that if they try they can get the customer to pay Rs 10,000 a month.

A ULIP or an endowment plan with Rs 10,000 per month as premium might give the buyer just Rs 10–15 lakh as insurance cover (typically 10x to 15x annual premium); a vastly inadequate sum compared to the 1 crore the person needs! But the seller persists and gets his way, largely because the customer has no idea how to work the metrics, and gets a feeling of happiness that there is some insurance and investment, when there really isn't.

In the longer term, I expect the tax benefits of insurance to go away. There are two areas to this – first, insurance proceeds of any sort are tax-free, even where the insurance cover is next to nothing and the product was primarily a product to save money. The second is a tax deduction on the amount invested every year, subject to an upper overall limit.

Both these tax breaks are under threat in the longer term, as the government tries to find new means of raising revenue to meet increasing deficits. Additionally, it's untenable that long-term savings of one nature – insurance or PF – are non-taxable, but buying long-dated government bonds or (non-equity) mutual funds makes you pay tax on the gains.

Lastly, if the government introduces a tax for inheritance (a proposal under discussion) then life insurance with a large one-time payment becomes an easy way to avoid such a tax. So I reckon it is quite likely that the government will plug the loophole sometime by making 'insurance as an investment' liable to tax.

My guess is, within a decade, we are likely to see the tax-free exit status of many schemes vanish or dwindle. At the least, this will force you to invest in low-yielding annuities if you want to retain a tax advantage. Put it another way: To assume that if I buy, I will not be charged a tax on exit even after twenty years is fraught with risk.

The last problem is that of complexity. Insurance products are incredibly complex, despite heavy regulation of the industry. Or maybe that's why they're complex because the insurer has to sidestep and find loopholes in the regulations.

Financial products are typically of two types – high risk, where the returns cannot be predicted in any reasonable manner, and low risk, where the return is either guaranteed or specified (the risk here is in whether the seller will go bust).

Equity is a high-risk proposition, while fixed deposit and other debt options are the second. Insurance products provide a mix and match, with some products giving a vague guarantee with an additional potential upside (like 50 per cent minimum guaranteed return or highest NAV in ten years).

Then they give you weird terms – you pay for five years, you can exit only after ten years, the guarantee applies on the first seven years' NAV, and so on. And then, if you die, the insurance might pay out the guaranteed amount, the 'sum assured', the amount that your investment has grown, or the lowest of all three.

By the time you understand the terms and are able to calculate your real return, you might find it ridiculously low (if your brain hasn't turned to jelly). A case in point: The real return on that '50 per cent in ten years guaranteed' cases is just short of 5 per cent per year, which is unacceptably low, even if you consider all the taxes saved.

Most people give up before they reach the 'real return' calculation – which is why insurers can easily stuff charges into such policies, knowing that if someone is silly enough to invest with a 5 per cent real return, he won't even know that they can take a significant chunk of money as commissions. While we have seen charges that added up to 50 per cent to 60 per cent of the first few years of premium, even the lower 10 per cent charges we see today are massive, compared to the 1 per cent to 3 per cent that are charged by, say, mutual funds.

The problem is that such products are sold – and sold hard – to customers. What we see in the life insurance industry is more of the industry and less of the insurance. And given that these policies increasingly suck the blood out of unwary buyers, there's less life as well.

'Forced saving'

I could go on and on about how insurance policies are horrible, but if you don't actually save your money, you will be left with nothing.

This is critical to understand. If you don't save, you won't grow. If you get too smart and try for maximum return, you will eventually be too scared to invest more, and then, just save too little.

Saving at 4 per cent a year, even if suboptimal, is better than not saving at all. Let's say I gave you two options:
(a) Put money in a high-risk equity portfolio that will go up and down but over the long term should do at least 10 per cent a year.
(b) Put money in a low-risk fixed deposit where you will only get 5 per cent a year.

Everyone has both these options, at all times. Yet, if you had Rs 1,00,000 you will put Rs 10,000 in the high-risk equity portfolio and Rs 90,000 in the low-risk one. Or just ask ten of your friends – more will choose (b) over (a).

But the behaviour in this respect gets even worse. People simply do not invest at all. They keep money in their savings accounts. And because it's available, they spend it. Or worse, someone asks for a loan, and they give it.

If you take the money out of a person's 'available' universe, from her savings account, then she can't spend it. It's a small mental nudge, that the money is not available for use. Therefore, you have to create a mechanism to move money out of savings accounts.

The simplest way is to just make a fixed deposit, but even those can be broken on demand. To take money even more strongly out of your hands, the insurance companies offer your products where you HAVE to wait five to ten years to get your money back.

This concept of 'forced saving' is a boon for many people who will otherwise not save at all. For those of you who find it difficult to avoid spending the money you can access, insurance policies are good. Even if they give you low returns, the fact is that they squirrel away the money for you when you wouldn't do so yourself.

Add to this the tax incentive for insurance, where, for the longest time, the rules say that you can avoid paying tax on any income that you direct to insurance plans (up to a given limit) and then, all proceeds of insurance are tax-free when you take it out.

Why is this bad? It's the mai-baap attitude. Some authority decided it's best your money is not accessible to you, because you are too stupid to avoid spending it. This sounds like they are trying to save you from yourself, which is a sign that we believe most people are immature and incapable of learning how to handle money better.

Think about it – why wait ten years? What if you need money in three years because of an emergency? You can't get it because one of the mai-baap types decided five years is the earliest you are allowed to have an emergency. As the great Rajinikanth would say: 'Five years, mind it!'

Suckered by the mai-baap

What's the alternative, you ask? The US seems to have a decent alternative concept for savings. This is the idea of a retirement account – an IRA. No tax when you put money in. Fully taxed when you take money out. So you let it grow, and there's no tax on the growth, and then when it's time for you to retire, you start taking money out slowly. When you do withdraw money from an IRA, there's a tax but there's not much other income for most retirees. So the tax paid stays low.

There's no mai-baap because:
- You can invest where you like – stocks, bonds, whatever.
- You can take out money when you like – just pay the tax on the money.
- No investment is more tax friendly than the alternatives.

Until such ideas come to India, insurance will continue to be mis-sold. The forced saving concept is illogical for those with even the slightest inclination to do better with their finances.

The ministry of mis-selling

The following open letters describe common mis-selling practices.

Have you mis-sold your ULIP today?

Dear Insurance Agent,

After the forced rejigging of ULIPs, you must be in dire straits in trying to sell insurance without gouging your customers' eyes out in the form of commissions. But do not despair. It is possible to make money in any situation, and this one is no different.

All you need is appropriate verbiage. You will tell people about the current plans offering so much more – up to 30 times their annual premium! Omit of course to tell them that for someone who can afford Rs 50,000 a year, the Rs 15 lakh cover offered is woefully inadequate – if they don't know that, why should you educate them?

And then you say the costs have dramatically reduced. From losing 75 per cent to 100 per cent of their first year's premium, they now lose ONLY 6 per cent in the first year, and at least 3 per cent in subsequent years. Don't bother to tell them that they will not pay such heavy charges in any other long term financial instrument, like mutual funds, NPS, or such hare-brained low-commission schemes.

Since you have to, you can mention that policy administration charge of 0.4 per cent per month as something they don't need to bother about – of course, in reality it's another 5 per cent a year that they lose. If a sucker is born every day, take him for everything he has. Hey, it's less than we used to charge earlier, if that's a consolation.

Selling ULIPs was easy, and now it has gotten only marginally more difficult. But that does not mean you should stop your mis-selling and cross over to the side of actually telling customers the truth. Told selectively and appropriately, you need not ever utter a lie, and still make your annual 'best mis-selling agent' trip to Bangkok a reality. Do not forget, of course, to pay your membership fees at the Ministry.

Best regards,

The Ministry of Mis-selling

Dear Real Estate Broker,

How many plots have you mis-sold recently? It is imperative that you continue the system of telling sheeple how fast the city of Delhi will expand towards Bhopal and thus sell those tiny plots of land in the Chambal valley. Sure, once in a while some dacoits come along, and there are no roads for at least 50 kilometres, but the India growth story will not stop.

In fact, we all know very well that certain key politicians, (whose names may not be mentioned but we can hint about who they are) are very close to signing a deal for a large property right there. You must continue with the noble habit of showing customers empty grasslands and telling them about the fancy new project that will emerge, sometime in the next decade.

Not that the customers expect to hold that long. Your customers are 'investors', a classic breed, who will first buy and then flip the property, allowing you to get repeated commissions from the same piece of real estate. All they need is the imperceptible nod of your head when you say a project will happen, and they'll fork out the Rs 5,00,000 advance to ensure you sucker them first.

And when you sell the apartments, be sure to mention the 1800 square foot 'super built-up area' which includes every piece of square footage in the complex and sometimes, square feet invented from pure imagination. After all, 1000 sq. ft carpet area ought to be enough for anyone; people will pay anything if it's 'super-built-up', even if it's not built up, nor super in any way.

You are not obligated to tell them about the charges that will inevitably come later – like the Rs 3 per square foot maintenance cost that hurts even after they own the property. Then there are the charges that the developer will invent to squeeze buyers like transfer charges, additional deficit charges, and we-just-want-some-money charges.

What if the developer vanishes with the money? Or real estate prices fall?
(Note: this part has been snipped by the censor board, because real estate prices can never fall)

As a conscientious real estate mis-seller, you should continue to highlight how India has a shortage of space, regardless of your knowledge of vast empty countryside and horrendously expensive urban real estate. Keep those opinions to yourself; just a few deals more and you will be able to afford an expensive piece of the pie yourself. But you'll still have to pay the maintenance charges.

Yours sincerely,
The Department of Overpriced Real Estate
The Ministry of Mis-selling

Dear Job Aspirant,
Have you embellished your résumé recently? If not, it is now time to consider doing so. Companies make so many undesirable

demands on recruits, such as actual experience in doing some of the things which you are obviously capable of but have never had the opportunity to do. Do not let this come in your way – invent such projects, or copy them from your friends' résumés. We know that companies have fallen so low as to actually ask questions about specific projects that you were not aware were even on your résumé, but you can always answer them by saying that was not in your specific area of operation. So, if you have written 'Java' on your résumé, and the interviewer asks you to declare an integer variable, you must immediately state that in your company, someone else declares variables and you only perform complex tasks such as the ISO-9001 documentation of who declared the variable and why.

You may feel squeamish every once in a while if you have a tender conscience, but let us assure you that you are in no way different from the companies that you are trying to work for. They, as you are well aware, tell customers they have ready staff who are extremely knowledgeable in, say, low-level chipsets when the only person on the project is you, whose deep experience with chips ends with Lay's Cheese and Onion.

Or, they tell you to bill eight hours to one client and six hours to another, when most of your four actual working hours were spent in meetings debating the colour of the Excel sheet in which to record these hours. What goes around must come around; a few white lies will not destroy the world, especially when it's the difference between a good salary and the lack of one.

Your comrade-in-arms,
The Department of Job Application,
The Ministry of Mis-selling

Footprints on the sands of time

> 'A person often meets his destiny on the road he took to avoid it.' – Jean de La Fontaine

Funnily enough, the above quote came to me through a recorded movie; I am not really fond of French poetry. But it triggered a thought – that this seems to be what we're doing in the whole financial world recently, and as an addition, it seems like we expect to die before we meet our destiny.

Take Aditya Birla Money (ABM). According to Forbes, ABM sold investors a 'risky options strategy' called Options Maxima as a safe investment; and later, when the market took a steep upturn, lost Rs 103 crore! The problem? The hopes of high returns for low risk. In the twelve months prior to September 2011, the market had stayed in a fairly narrow trading range, so it had been very profitable to write 'option strangles'. These are positions that make money if the market stays within a narrow range but lose an unlimited amount if it moves beyond that range.

Dating back as far as October 2009, I have heard of brokers and high net worth individuals doing this as a planned strategy – writing strangles, such that they made some money if the Nifty stayed within a range as wide as 4000 on the lower side, to 6000 on the upper side. With the Nifty firmly ensconced in the 4800 to 5300 trading range, they made money for a number of months, and the strategy seemed like shooting ducks in a barrel.

Since then, multiple financial products have come forth with such a strategy, and as happens when everyone piles on to the same concept, the yield on the trade dropped drastically.

The response? Use a narrower range, and leverage by borrowing the capital for the trade to get higher returns. Eventually in September 2011, the Nifty shot up way beyond the range. When it crossed the 6000 level, these option strangles lost enormous amounts – even more so because they were highly leveraged, which meant they also had to pay interest on the money they lost! If they were less leveraged, they wouldn't make the return they wanted – upwards of 2 per cent a month – and which the brokers 'nearly guaranteed' because, look, this strategy hasn't lost money for a year.

It doesn't really take a black swan event to unravel concepts like this. A black swan is an event that you couldn't foresee from the known past, reflecting the belief that swans were synonymous with the colour white until the day a black variety was seen.

The Nifty move of about 11 per cent in a month as occurred in September 2011 wasn't a black swan. In May 2009, for example, election furore took the Nifty from 3600 to 4200 in one day. That move triggered market circuit breakers on the upside. Ignore that?

Well, in October 2007, there was a 10 per cent downmove in a single day. And again in January 2008. And once more in October 2008. If large moves have happened overnight four times in two years, and you have a strategy that loses big amounts of money on large moves, it is both misleading and foolish to describe it as 'safe'.

Graeco-Irish stew

Ireland asked for a bailout a few years ago. The nation wanted to fund its beleaguered banks, whose debts were way higher than their assets. The reason Irish banks were in trouble was that they offered cheap credit that funded a housing bubble, which crashed.

The bailout, though, is not just of the institutions in Ireland. In an indirect way, money was being borrowed to pay back foreign holders of Irish bank bonds. In effect, the Irish state is insolvent. So adding the bailout money to Ireland's existing government debt at the 5 per cent interest rate Greece got will render Ireland bankrupt in a few years. To an observer, it seems like the Irish have kicked the can a little bit further down the road.

It was a choice between letting Ireland go down – and handle the potentially massive consequences to non-Irish banks and countries – or fund Ireland to the tune of around 100 billion euros to let it last a little longer and hope the world ends before it goes down again. For investors, it might seem like a low-risk trade: Let's all invest in European country bonds because, hey, everyone's getting bailed out, so we'll surely get our money back.

The bailout Greece got earlier was also 100 billion euros. Like the saying goes, famously misattributed to Senator Dirksen, 'A billion here, a billion there, and pretty soon you're talking real money.'

During a trip to Goa, I was at the casinos, watching and playing a more sober version of the stock market. The games are terribly against you in terms of odds. Casino games are engineered in such a way that you think you have a good chance, but if you play long enough, you will surely lose. If you want the thrill of playing in a casino play only for stakes you are happy to lose, and if you win, continue making the same bet sizes, or just walk away.

But the thrill of looking at big wins by customers often overshadows the gloom and despair of the losses. Those are justified by 'I had a great time anyway'. This 'win-win' feeling is cleverly magnified by casino authorities using various bells and chimes for attracting attention to winners and paying up in cash (people associate big wads of cash with lots of money, when a single sheet of paper may be worth far more). You then emotionally justify playing more – after all, you will win sometime, and on the downside it's just a little more money. A billion here, a billion there . . .

Chasing low risk is fine, but anything that shows high returns for abnormally low risk should be viewed with suspicion. As a rule of thumb, anything that gives you higher returns than the best bank deposit you can find probably involves some levels of risk and these risks may be cleverly hidden. Understanding risk is a complex concept – and it's better to take a simple product if you don't have the time to analyse something in detail, or understand that there may be better alternative products with the same risk profile.

In my view, there is nothing like a zero-risk investment – as people holding outer European debt discovered. Russian debt holders discovered in 1998 that even government debt paid in local currency (rubles) was not beyond risk, even when the government has the power to print money. That crisis took down Nobel Prize winners. In that context, nothing is risk-free, really. We must, in my opinion, embrace risk for what it is – the door to a higher return, and use just enough money so we can come and knock again tomorrow.

If we keep thinking about how bad the world is, and that nothing is risk-free, we will despair of living in a world not worth investing in. Instead, it's best to think everything is a game of chance, like that minesweeper game where, on that first click, you hope and pray that there isn't a bomb underneath. Unlike real minesweepers though, you do get to play again – and that must be our spirit going forward. Win more when we win, lose less when we lose, and stay in the game.

The Goa trip introduced me to another poem, courtesy my more knowledgeable cousin, by W.H. Longfellow. A few of the passages that I absolutely loved:

> Tell me not in mournful numbers,
> 'Life is but an empty dream!'
> For the soul is dead that slumbers,
> And things are not what they seem.
> ...
> Lives of great men all remind us
> We can make our lives sublime,
> And, departing, leave behind us
> Footprints on the sands of time;

The pain that is real estate

You have to own a house, they tell you. Because you have to. And then a number of reasons are given.

You won't get a good 'bride' in an arranged marriage, some people told me, if you don't own a house. It's a badge of achievement, they say, not realizing that the badge is equivalent to a banker's noose around your neck for the next twenty years.

Or 'Why do you pay rent, when you can pay a monthly instalment and just own the house outright?'

Financially, this doesn't make sense. A three-bedroom apartment in South Bengaluru sells for about Rs 1.2 crore in

2021. The monthly instalment on a twenty-year loan is about Rs 1 lakh a month.

The rent, for that same house, will be about Rs 30,000 a month. You could pay rent and take a fancy holiday every month if you give up the 'badge' of owning a house.

But house prices go up, don't they? You might be paying now, but you'll save so much that you'll have rupee bills flying around you in a decade. This again is another way to sucker you.

The lost decade

Housing prices between 2010 and 2021 have hardly changed. I've lived in three cities – Mumbai, Gurugram and Bengaluru, and in all of them prices are roughly the same as they were in 2010. In effect, you'd pay interest on your loan for ten years. That's more than the rent you would have paid, and yet, after all that time, you have no gains.

There are good reasons for this. There's a lot of housing out there, especially in the 'luxury' level. There's more supply than demand. This meant prices did not rise too much.

There's also the phenomenon of urbanization. People in urban areas want mobility. If you rent, you don't have to tether yourself to a locality. Moving jobs? Move house as well. Moving cities? No problem. Worldwide, urban areas have low homeownership. New York, for example, has about 51 per cent homeownership (measured by the percentage of houses where owners live, versus renters). India has 87 per cent homeownership, by the way. Even urban areas are upwards of 70 per cent.

Still, we're all pushed to buy homes, mostly because people feel prices will just keep going up. Indeed, they do tend to go up in many areas.

Why real estate prices don't fall easy

Why are real estate prices not falling much? The answer, they'll tell you, is that costs are so much that it doesn't make sense to cut prices. Or that anyhow, 'circle rates' are this much and prices can't fall below.

Some of these reasons are partially true. Let's say I'm a builder. I have taken a loan to build a complex of, say, 500 flats. For this, I've spent about Rs 150 crore buying the land, another Rs 150 crore for permissions and basic construction, and roughly Rs 100 crore in interiors. I've sold about 350 houses for Rs 1 crore each. I still owe the bank Rs 150 crore for the loan I took, including interest.

To be able to get back Rs 150 crore I must sell at Rs 1 crore per flat, or I'll make a loss, I tell you. But this is just developers misstating things. The reason the loan still has Rs 150 crore on it is that the builder used Rs 50 crore somewhere in the middle to buy another chunk of real estate. Account for that, and the price can be cut 50 per cent if the intention was to only pay the bank back.

Further, there's no law that says the builders' profits are guaranteed! Ask a kirana shop owner: If he buys 100 soaps at a bulk price and the brands are not selling, he will just offer a discount and sell at a loss. There's a cost to having non-selling soaps sitting in a shop, because they take up valuable space. Take a loss, move on.

When a builder can't sell at a lower price, his losses add up because interest is being charged on the outstanding loans. It's better for the builder to sell and pay up, compared to paying even higher interest.

But why is everyone against prices falling? The answer is more complex.

A big factor is that current owners and buyers don't want prices to fall. Imagine an under-construction project when you've paid Rs 8000 per sq. ft, and the builder cuts it to Rs 6000 to just get it out of his system.

You'll protest and demand that your price be cut too.

That is simply unsustainable. If you've agreed to pay Rs 8000, then further price cuts are not automatically yours by right. But people will withhold further payments in the hope they can negotiate a lower price. That delays the project, which needs the payments to put the finishing touches.

This screws things up for everyone involved.

And then there are the flippers. If builders cuts rates, they can't sell their flats which they intended to after some time, and the builders have depended on such people to build offtake in many projects. So there is some gratitude and prior relationships to deal with when it comes to flippers.

But this might be more nuanced too – the flippers don't want to take possession.

The concept is this: If you're flipping an apartment, you buy early, and the property isn't actually ready. So, what do you get? Only an agreement to construct this property. The property, then is not actually yours yet – you will own it only after the builder hands over 'possession'.

An 'investor' (whose idea was to buy at the construction stage and then sell) had what seemed like a unique problem when I spoke with him:

Investor: I have this property in Mumbai, it's ready but I don't want possession.

Me: Why not? You've paid good money for it, why not just take it?

Investor: Look, if he gives me possession, I have to pay monthly maintenance from now on. I have to pay to register the property (roughly 5 per cent to 7 per cent of value). Or I have to find a buyer, and there's no buyer for that flat at my purchase price. No way, I hope we are delayed further.

This was solid, if contrarian, logic. It was eye-opening since it seemed so perverse at first glance. Due to such buyers, the builder's under pressure to actually not complete the project. If you had bought a house, you might take possession since you want to live there, but because of investors who want to flip without taking on additional costs, the project may take much longer to complete.

The government doesn't like lower revenue either, so it will not allow registrations at rates far lower than circle rates, though they now allow for 10 per cent lower prices. And circle rates will not correct down either: Imagine a government official being held responsible for bringing revenue down!

Brokers don't also like it – but they play a part in silent 'distress' deals. Let the builder keep high shelf prices, but do a side-deal negotiation at a much lower price for a few people. This is not good for business as distress is not scalable. But at least it's something.

In general, the only people who want lower prices are those that want to buy and live in a house. And even those people don't want continuously falling prices after they buy.

The same philosophy doesn't apply to cars. Houses are a more prized asset.

This all comes back to one thing: Real estate prices crash only in a deep crisis, when these considerations are thrown to the wind because cash is needed desperately by a few people.

That need cascades and becomes a lot of people selling to beat the rush to the exit. Real estate is much more about emotional behaviour than about pure supply and demand.

It's not like crashes haven't happened. Prices crashed 50 per cent in most large cities in the mid-1990s. Even more in the suburbs. The massive glut of houses in Asiad Village in Delhi that were built for athletes in the 1982 Asian Games, and placed for sale after the event, meant that prices in Delhi crashed hard. So hard, in fact, that public sector banks that funded the Asian Games Complex construction ended up owning these houses in lieu of their loans. Those did make them a fortune a few decades later as prices went up, eventually. But prices can crash heavily, when there is a crisis.

Don't leave any amount outstanding on your credit card

Let's say you have a credit bill of Rs 20,100 due on 1 May. And you paid Rs 20,000. You're thinking 'Oh, 3 per cent a month but only on Rs 100, no? I can pay.'

You're in for a big surprise.

Your bill date was probably 20 April. After that, you would have had some Swiggy bills, some other purchases, etc. on the cars. That's, say, another Rs 11,000.

You'll get charged 3 per cent on the Rs 100 you didn't pay the last time, sure.

You'll also get charged 3 per cent for the Rs 11,000!

Once you have an outstanding amount left after the due date, even one rupee, you pay interest from the day you transacted. Even if that transaction was BEFORE the due date.

Also, any MORE transactions attract interest from day one.

If you were unaware and bought some Rs 9000 worth of items on 10 May. Now you have Rs 20,100 outstanding. Each purchase is charged interest from the day you purchased it.

So on your next bill on 20 May, you'll see an interest charge of about Rs 600.

They also add GST, so you pay nearly Rs 800 extra. Your bill is now Rs 21,000.

Just because you 'revolved' Rs 100.

If you can't pay on any month, please do not revolve your loans. Ask your bank – or just about any bank – for a personal loan, which will be far cheaper than this (and there's no GST on interest on a personal loan).

And get credit card balance to zero. ASAP.

Also there are start-ups offering loans at lower rates, and you should absolutely use these as opportunities to cut down your credit card outstanding to zero.

The purpose of a credit card 'revolve' facility is to steal from you, so don't let them.

What if you can't pay?
You may have certain circumstances when you cannot pay. Talk to your bank, or to other personal loan companies, that will give you a personal loan. Use that to pay your credit card bill.

Note that if you have been revolving credit on your card, the new lender will know. It's part of your credit score. So you can't avoid them knowing. But remember, credit cards charge over 36 per cent a year! It's 3 per cent or more per month, which actually is ludicrously high. Plus GST, which means the net cost to you is about 50 per cent a year if you revolve on the card.

Instead, pay off the card in full by borrowing from a different loan. Sell your investments if you have any. Use them to pay back the card. You shouldn't be investing if you don't have enough to pay the credit card debt – if you must borrow, ensure you can borrow at far lower costs.

Often, people feel ashamed of themselves for having credit card outstanding amounts, and will not want to reveal this to friends or family. This is not a good idea, because all you will do is allow extremely high interest rates to accumulate and compound. Effectively you are giving in to moneylenders just like illiterate poor do. Credit cards are nasty moneylenders in suits. You have an option: Work to ensure you don't pay them those crazy interest rates.

The Nirav Modi scam

There's a huge 'fraud' at Punjab National Bank, which involves a lot of lies by a lot of people. Here's where we try to explain what we think happened.

The scam, and how it stands

Punjab National Bank announced a big fraud of Rs 11,000 crore-plus in a surprise letter to the stock exchanges on 14 February 2018.

Then it shot off a message to a bunch of banks, blaming a now retired employee for raising fraudulent Letters of Undertaking (LoUs) for over six years. This blamed the people who received the funds, companies owned by a jeweller named Nirav Modi and, in another case, those owned by Mehul Choksi. This is the publicly listed Gitanjali Gems. Nirav Modi is Choksi's nephew. (Trivia: Nirav Modi's brother, Nishal, is married to Isheta

Salgaokar, who's Dhirubhai Ambani's granddaughter through his daughter, Dipti.)

So what actually happened?

First, the Concept

Let's understand how things work in the import–export business.

Some importer, let's call him Nirav Modi or NM, wants to import pearls or diamonds and then sell them after adding value by making fancy designer jewellery. The purchase requires money. So NM approaches a bank, say Punjab National Bank (PNB).

PNB says, look, I'll give you a loan but it will be at 10 per cent.

NM thinks hard and says, 'No, that's too much. Wait, why don't I take a foreign currency loan instead, after all I'm buying in dollars? Much lower interest rates, no? I can get this at LIBOR+2 per cent and LIBOR is like 1.5 per cent so I'll have the money at 3.5 per cent!' (The London Interbank Offered Rate or LIBOR is a standard benchmark interest rate for hard currency loans.)

But who will give NM a foreign currency loan? A bank abroad? They don't know NM. They don't have any history of dealing with NM, so why will they give him money?

So NM goes to PNB and says, 'Boss, you're my banker, so please help me convince some foreign bank to give me some money to buy diamonds. Say that you will guarantee my loan by giving me a n LOU.'

PNB now should be saying, 'Look, if you want us to give Rs 100 crore guarantee, you give me stuff worth Rs 110 crore at least as collateral.'

But PNB, for some strange reason, doesn't ask for collateral at all. More on that later.

So now the foreign bank is ready to lend NM the money since PNB will guarantee it. The foreign bank trusts PNB. Why does it trust PNB?

First of all, it trusts PNB because it's a scheduled commercial bank, which means it's regulated by the RBI. Also, the majority shareholder is the Government of India. That means PNB will meet its commitments unless India goes bust.

So PNB sends a message on SWIFT – the banking message service – that PNB guarantees Rs 100 crore for 180 days for Mr NM at an interest rate of, say, LIBOR + 2 per cent. It's like a message – written in stone, effectively – that says PNB will pay, if NM doesn't pay.

The foreign bank trusts only PNB – it doesn't know or care who NM is, or what NM is doing with the money. So it transfers the money to PNB's account. This by the way is called a 'nostro' – an account that a bank like PNB maintains with banks abroad, where the other bank can send money meant for PNB customers.

PNB's nostro account receives the money. PNB then gives NM the money from the nostro account. Or rather, this is usually sent directly to pay off whoever NM is buying his diamonds from. This payment is to someone outside India usually, to fund the purchase.

Note this carefully: The other bank puts money in PNB's nostro account. It doesn't give it to NM. It only knows that PNB has given a guarantee on the SWIFT inter-banking channel.

Note: The other bank may well be a foreign branch of an Indian bank. Meaning, the lender might even be PNB's own branch in, say, Belgium, lending to NM through PNB's nostro account with it. After a while, the overseas banks have realized something unsettling – they have figured out that PNB's guarantee is a strange beast that isn't backed with much. But we'll come to that later.

The foreign bank couldn't care less about whether NM was buying diamonds or bitcoin – to them PNB is the borrower.

Why does PNB give a guarantee? Fees. A bank may charge up to 2 per cent a year to give an LoU.

So what happens when it's time to pay back?

NM has to receive the pearls or diamonds in India, sell them in India or abroad, receive the money and pay PNB in India. On the due date written on the LoU.

Then PNB will pay back the foreign bank saying, 'Okay, we got the customer's money so we're giving it back to you.' This is with interest, etc., on whatever terms were agreed between PNB and the foreign bank.

That's what is supposed to happen. But in reality, things went berserk.

The reality: Enter the Ponzi.

NM might not pay back at all. NM might use the money to speculate in the markets. Or do something else.

What if NM in the above example simply didn't have the money to pay back? Instead, he asks a PNB official to open *ANOTHER LoU*. For the amount owed, plus interest. So if we had the first LoU at $10 million, the second one is $11 million to cover interest on the first.

The money from the second LoU is used to repay the first. It's just rolling over of the credit. Rinse and repeat. Over and over. This is the standard definition of a Ponzi scheme.

This can easily balloon into larger amounts, so large that it's too much to handle. In effect many such arrangements have turned into Ponzi schemes, with one LoU being opened to repay another, and so on.

But won't the bank know it's given two loans and then gotten repaid for only one?

In this case, it didn't. There was a problem. A rogue employee allegedly started to send the SWIFT messages without putting the requisite entries into the core PNB banking system. So no one in PNB supposedly got to know there was so much outstanding.

The following sequence of events is what is likely to have happened.

It looks like:

- Nirav Modi took loans from foreign branches of Indian banks through an LoU issued by PNB.
- This was done through a SWIFT-based LoU issued through a rogue employee (or many rogues) at PNB.
- The orders never showed up in the core PNB banking system for monitoring.
- LoUs were rolled over all the way from 2011, and naturally increased over time.
- The 'rogue official' retired in 2017. His replacement refused to roll over the LoU which came due in January 2018, because he couldn't find records of the past transactions in the system.
- No rollover means a default, since there was no money to pay. So PNB quickly filed an FIR, saying, 'Oh goodness! We have lost Rs 280 crore on the January 2018 LoUs.'
- Then someone said, 'Abeyaar, are there more of these not-in-system LoUs? Someone check, no?'
- Then someone checked.

- Oh Gawd! Rs 11,400 crore and counting.
- That's a lot of crore.
- Everyone in the bank panicked.

Why couldn't Nirav Modi just pay it back? He must have the original money, no?

If it was ever intended to be paid back, the rollovers wouldn't have been required. At some point, things got so out of hand that rollovers were required in order to just stay current.

Typically this would not be a problem. If PNB had done things right, they would have had collateral worth the amount of guarantee, and they would have sold the collateral and paid the foreign bank.

But, and here's another big issue: PNB didn't have any collateral.

Why did PNB give a guarantee without collateral?

If you and I go for a loan to a bank, they'll ask us for income proof, and collateral. Only small, tiny personal loans and credit card loans come backed without collateral. For something of the order of Rs 11,000 crore you would think they may ask for collateral. This is especially true after the affair with Vijay Mallya where loans to Kingfisher were given on nearly no collateral (though even there, there was a house and promoter shares pledged).

Why did PNB give this guarantee? It's typical of the way banks do this import–export business. Banks give guarantees for much more than the amount given as collateral (or they ask for no collateral) when there's a 'business relationship', etc. This is because 'nearly every bank' is doing it.

Importantly, the loan was not a 'fund-based limit'. In a fund-based limit like a term loan, the bank pays out money. In non-fund-based limits, the bank will only pay if someone else defaults, or a specified event happens. A bank guarantee, or an LC, or an LoU is non-fund based.

PNB assumed the foreign bank was giving a loan directly to Nirav Modi and that PNB needed to pay only in case Nirav Modi defaulted. So in the eyes of PNB it was always a 'non-fund-based' loan.

This is how a significant part of import financing works. All importers roll over credit, and they all use LoUs for much higher amounts than they offer as collateral.

The scale is huge. For every Rs 100 a bank has collateral, it will easily provide LoUs for up to 6x the amount. This is a real problem – most public sector banks do not keep much collateral against non-fund-based limits given to importing customers.

So even if a bank has collateral, it's nowhere near enough to cover the actual amount of the LoU. And such unfunded liabilities are not even mandatorily reported to the RBI!

Basel reporting: No disclosure

PNB has 'unfunded' exposure of Rs 11,000 crore, it claims. But they don't even reveal it in their Basel III disclosure:
- The funded exposure to 'Gems and Jewellery' is *shown at Rs 1860 crore.*
- *Unfunded to the same sector: Rs 842 crore.*

This doesn't even add up. So, in effect, PNB didn't reveal that it was funding massive quantities of 'unfunded, contingent exposure'. It will, of course, pretend that it didn't know, because the transactions weren't in the core banking system.

Did employees hide it? Was PNB responsible or was it a fraud?

Can employees be responsible? Could they have hidden the credit and the rolling over of LoUs? Honestly, how does a Rs 11,000 crore credit pass muster without top management realizing it? For comparison, PNB made a total income of Rs 48,000 crore in the year ending March 2017 – this implies it had a gigantic 20 per cent of its entire revenues sitting in one unseen sinkhole.

Think of it – your nostro account with these other banks keeps getting big credits that add up to Rs 11,000 crore. There's something very wrong if you do not reconcile it in the accounting. The basic question 'Why is this money even here?' should have been asked by someone auditing the accounts surely? SWIFT messages are of a very specific kind. Why wouldn't PNB audit the SWIFT trail and reconcile it with the core banking system? How many more such skeletons will tumble out if they perform this basic task?

Their excuses are:
- Data wasn't entered into the core banking system. (Of course, otherwise you would have had to report it.)
- LoUs weren't authorized. (Hard to believe, because the amounts are so very large. Surely someone at the top would have to know?)
- The SWIFT system was illegally used. (Again, hard to believe that a bank like PNB would not audit its SWIFT messages regularly. Or its auditors. Or the RBI.)

It's a mystery how seniors in the bank failed to spot this. We may probably never know the full story and if there is anyone else in the bank other than the jailed PNB employee who was involved.

Fees wise: Imagine Rs 11,000 crore worth of LoUs being renewed each year – that's up to Rs 200 crore in fees coming to PNB's top line. You could bribe an employee to maybe give you a small increase – say, even Rs 10–20 crore. But when you hit numbers like Rs 11,000 crore this is something top management should have known.

What's the scale of this scam?

While PNB reported it as a Rs 11,000 crore scam, they filed an FIR with the CBI for only Rs 280 crore. This has probably expanded since then but even if the total outstanding is as much as that, there's a good chance that the actual loss will be less.

All of it will be borne by PNB. Whether someone abused its SWIFT usage is not relevant, if PNB's SWIFT message said it will pay, it has to pay if there is a default.

But think about the fallout. The problem was that some liabilities were not in the system. There could be more such LoUs. From the same branch, or others. Other banks could have such 'unknown' LoUs too. It's trivial to start looking for this – and when people do, it's guaranteed that Nirav Modi will not be an isolated case.

Why did the limits have no collateral behind them? If all banks are told to verify their non-fund-based limits and demand collateral against them (say, at least 25 per cent) then the scale of this high-risk practice would be seen to be absolutely massive.

If Nirav Modi and Mehul Choksi are extradited to India too, we might discover more about this scam and it's likely that similar scams are still running undetected in other banks. A very large number of importers of commodities have been indulging is such practices to rotate credit. Tighter regulation here could change the game dramatically for every other bank with importer accounts in the Indian financial system.

One simple point is that this particular set of transactions will result in lower losses than Rs 11,000 crore for PNB because there will be recoveries. But if the RBI asks all banks to demand collateral on such non-fund lending, and to stop these practices of issuing LoUs without collateral, the scale will be seen to be many times larger than Rs 11,000 crore.

There is never just one cockroach in a sewer. When you dig deeper into the banking system, you are likely to find more in the way of dirty, dark secrets.

It's amazing that our banks have been this lax, but that's because they have been allowed to be. No bankers have been investigated, the rot inside has been ignored and industrialists have instead been the target of outrage. It's time to look at banks as malicious players too, and to fix that rot.

NSEL: The deficit of trust

An innocuous-looking notification from the Forward Markets Commission (FMC) appeared on 12 July 2013. It caused an earthquake in the offices of the National Spot Exchange Limited (NSEL), a commodities exchange promoted by the Financial Technologies India Limited (FTIL) group led by Jignesh Shah.

The notification restricted NSEL from making fresh contracts available as the exchange was likely in contravention of the Forwards Contracts Regulation Act. NSEL first changed its contract duration to comply, and then, when it found customers leaving in droves, threw up its arms and shut down the exchange.

More than Rs 5500 crore was due, and over the next few days it became evident that there was neither the money nor the underlying 'spot' goods to settle outstanding trades by over 15,000 investors.

The scale of this default dwarfs the last big exchange crisis, the Rs 600 crore settlement problem at the Calcutta Stock Exchange in 2001.

Let's try and decode what the whole thing was about.

What is a spot exchange?

Commodity spot trading is about buying and selling a commodity, paying cash for and receiving your goods on the 'spot'. 'Spot' signifies that the buyer and seller agree on a price and 'deliver' their side of the contract immediately – or close to immediately.

When you buy rice at your local kirana shop you pay 'spot' and take the rice also. If you buy online, you pay on the spot and receive the rice when the delivery person comes home, a little while later. We'll still call it a spot contract.

NSEL was a spot exchange designed to help with this activity. It had the added feature of being electronic (so buyers and sellers can be in different locations) and anonymous (the buyer and seller don't know who the other side is, but the exchange does).

The important feature of any such exchange is that the exchange has to stand guarantor to both parties to ensure the contract is settled. If you want to buy online, and you aren't sure that the online website will actually deliver the goods, you won't buy there.

If the buyer says he'll buy but doesn't actually pay – such as a credit card default, for example – the exchange should effectively stand guarantee and pay the seller regardless. It's a similar exercise if the seller defaults – the exchange will return the money to the buyer. Sometimes this is done by the exchange becoming the counterparty in each transaction; it buys whatever is being sold and sells it on to the buyer and does so instantly, matching all the trades (and taking a fee).

Now, when the seller and buyer are far away, how does the exchange guarantee delivery of physical goods? The seller must deposit his goods in an exchange-designated warehouse. These goods are then tested and verified for quality and weight, etc., and a warehouse receipt (WR) is given to be used for electronic trading. Once you have a WR, you say: 'Come buy this from me, and the warehouse will send you the goods.'

When something is sold, the WR is electronically transferred to the buyer; this receipt entitles the buyer to remove the goods or to retain the goods there (to sell them later) by paying warehouse rental charges.

The rules governing commodity trading were at the time, regulated by the Forward Market Commission (FMC). Under the Forward Contracts Regulation Act, any contract called 'spot' must be settled within eleven days. That is, both delivery of goods and transfer of money must happen within eleven days (called 'T+11').

The eleven days give the buyer and seller time to complete the contract. Thus, this is not a 'forward' contract.

Forwards are like this: I'll buy rice from you next month (you haven't even harvested yet). But when you do harvest, I'll buy. You don't have the rice, so I give you a small advance and then 'settle' the contract when you do have the rice. Forward contracts have different standards of governance and regulation, because they involve promises that must be kept, and we know how well that goes in India if you don't wield a big stick. Forward contracts usually charge a higher price for the same goods because at the least there's an interest cost (called 'cost of carry') to be covered.

Spot contracts, by their nature, were deemed to be exempted from FMC regulation by a small notification in 2007, made by the Department of Consumer Affairs. This exemption was given specifically for one-day-duration contracts – technically contracts that complete both delivery of goods and transfer of money within two days, called 'T+2'.

What NSEL really did

Instead of just making T+2 contracts, the spot exchange designed multiple contracts. Some of them were T+2 settled, making them 'spot'. Others were the same product but settled after twenty-five to thirty-five days, called T+25 and T+36 contracts respectively. This was illegal – such contracts are forward contracts and NSEL was not authorized to execute these. But it did and no one stopped it.

Until the abuse of this system came to light. NSEL sold what seemed to be 'arbitrage'. You could 'buy' the T+2 contract (paying money) and 'sell' the T+25 contract (receiving money) and the difference in prices gave you nearly 15 per cent a year, annualized. Effectively, you would be the owner of half a ton of sugar, or castor seeds, or some such commodity, for about twenty-five days, before you did a reverse trade.

Think of it. You buy 500 kg of sugar at Rs 100 a kg in the spot contract. You sell the same 500 kg in the T+25 contract, at Rs 102. You make Rs 2 a kg of sugar, for a month, or 2 per cent. Net of transaction costs, you still get 1.25 per cent a month. And you don't actually have to own the sugar – you just leave it at the warehouse to be delivered to the next buyer.

The NSEL practically removed all constraints from investors – the goods would lie in the same warehouse and be sold from there, and the price difference included approximately 15 per cent net return a year after storage charges, VAT, etc.

This arbitrage was almost 'guaranteed'. NSEL as the exchange stood guarantee, or so investors thought, if they traded the prices right.

Many brokers peddled this product to their customers for over two years. The number of customers ballooned to over 15,000, each of whom put in at least Rs 2 lakh to get their 'superior' returns. After all, a sure-shot, no-risk 15 per cent a year is pretty impressive.

What was the problem?

Who was on the other side? Who was offering a good 15 per cent a year? That's the question no one was asking.

Was the arbitrage genuine? It appears not. The contracts were always sold in pairs. Brokers have reported no one was allowed by the exchange to take only one side of any contract – you always had to have a 'buy' on the near contract and a 'sell' on the far side, or vice versa.

A quick look at the Kadi contract for castor seeds, sold in pairs of T+3 and T+36, shows identical volumes and interest for both contracts in January 2013, and that's the case with every NSEL commodity that had both a near and far contract. This sort of matching is hardly possible in a normal market, so it confirms these contracts were always executed in pairs.

Think about it. Imagine I'm on the other side. I first sell you sugar at Rs 100, and then buy it back at Rs 102 a month later. You never even see the sugar. Replace 'sugar' with 'castles in the air' and you would still do this trade.

The Ponzi scheme

The question is: Why am I paying you 15 per cent? Why would anyone sell you something at 100 and buy back at 102 a month later?

It turns out now that those on the other side were just twenty-four members of the exchange, called planters, or processors, or borrowers. These members owned plants that processed commodities – or, at least, they claimed they did. For instance, NK Proteins owned a plant to process castor seeds in Kadi, Gujarat. The contract – the Kadi Castor Seeds contract – was settled at an NSEL warehouse located inside the Kadi plant of NK Proteins.

Did it have castor seeds at all? Who cares? Buy at Rs 100, sell at Rs 102!

Processors like NK Proteins (and there were twenty-three other such members) were on the other side of the trade. They would sell at T+2 and buy back at T+23, offering huge returns.

The fact that the contracts were executed in pairs indicates a financing programme. Something is being placed as collateral to borrow money for a short period. This used to be commonly known as 'badla financing' in the pre-2000 stock exchanges, where shares were used as collateral. (Badla is banned now; financing by this method has moved to the futures and options market.)

Let's say I am a plant owner, and I can't get a loan from a bank. I can effectively borrow from you at 18–24 per cent – much cheaper than I can borrow from the banks. And if I'm smart, I know that the goods I sell you will remain at a warehouse inside my premises, so why not cheat a little? I tell you, 'Yes, I've added more goods to your warehouse,' and you, on the other end of the phone, agree to this circular process.

In effect, I can invent stock that doesn't exist and borrow against it for fifteen days; I might pay some interest out, but I immediately get cash back in a new contract when I add even more imaginary stock. So I keep rolling over. This was the Ponzi game.

Indeed, it turned out that some of these twenty-four companies had weak balance sheets incapable of servicing large loans of Rs 900 crore, or so. The exchange facilitated this sort of financing, rather than putting a stop to it.

Most 'investors' rolled over their contracts. That is, when the contract was unwound after T+35, they would enter a fresh round of T+2 (buy) and T+35 (sell). Meaning, the interest received was also being ploughed back into further 'purchases'; a 'borrower', on the other hand, was pretending to pay interest, but was simply creating warehouse receipts for the interest, and trading them on the exchange, rolling over the contract forever.

If someone started doing this at Rs 100, and rolled over at Rs 102, Rs 104 etc. month after month, then in two years, this might easily become 150. No one would care.

Until everyone had to take notice.

The end of the game

All this had to stop sometime, and the circular from FMC stopped it. By disallowing the T+35 kind of contracts. You could do T+10, and that was it, the notification said.

First, on 16 July, the contract tenures were cut to T+10. Carrying out the same scheme at T+10 would involve too many pair trades – up from one a month to three a month, driving up transaction costs.

Next, some investors smelt a rat and didn't roll over their contracts at this point. So the system broke down

The lack of a rollover shuttered the exchange. When 'borrowers' were told that they had to pay back all the money, they simply could not (or didn't want to). And it turned out they didn't have the goods to back it up either.

On 31 July, NSEL issued a circular saying all future contracts would be stopped. And because there was a settlement problem, they would have to delay payouts for a while.

Remember, some investors had bought goods on a T+2 contract, paying upfront. Now they expected that after their twenty-five to thirty-five days, the other contract would kick in and they would be paid back money at the higher rate on that contract.

At this point, the exchange had to shell out since the buyers could invoke the guarantees. That's the role of an exchange. But because it didn't get paid from the borrowers, NSEL didn't have the capacity to pay up.

Lies, deceit and an incestuous web

The exchange started to lie. The CEO, Anjani Sinha, said on 1 August that they had a 'Settlement Guarantee Fund' of over Rs 800 crore and they had all the stocks in the NSEL warehouses. In a few days they changed that position, stating they had only Rs 60 crore in cash and the rest of the 'guarantee fund' was in stock. All entities were supposed to put a tiny amount – up to 5 per cent – as margin until trade completion. This, too, was unavailable for some reason.

Then, after telling everyone that they would get their money back, the NSEL management said they had to auction stock to get the money. Soon, even that avenue was seen to be a dead end since there wasn't any stock.

Jignesh Shah, the founder of FTIL, which promoted the exchange, said in a press conference that they would have a high-powered committee, including an ex-SEBI chief, a senior police officer and the like, to ensure settlements happen. As it turns out, the committee was useless at actually enforcing the contracts.

NSEL next created a complex settlement programme. After a few days, NSEL management offered a 'settlement calendar' stretching thirty weeks where people would be paid back Rs 174 crore a week for twenty weeks, Rs 86 crore a week after that, and a big balloon payment at the end.

NSEL couldn't even make the first week's payments properly – it paid up just half. In the second week, to fend off investor aggression, FTIL dipped into its resources and paid Rs 177 crore to settle those contracts with less than Rs 10 lakh outstanding. By 3 September, four weeks after the promise of Rs 174 crore a week, only Rs 15 crore more was paid.

In the middle of all of this, it turned out that many of NSEL's twenty-four processor members were related to each other. One of the biggest borrowers, NK Proteins, is owned by the son-in-law of NSEL's chairman Shankarlal Guru. Then there was the Indian Bullion Market Association, owned primarily by NSEL, which participated as a member, allowing parties in the bullion space to buy through them.

The whole thing began to stink to high heaven.

N. Sundaresha Subramanian of *Business Standard* visited many of the defaulting members and discovered strange things. There was a mall standing in the place where 2 lakh tons of sugar was supposedly stored, at the address of an NSEL borrower called Mangla Shree Properties. In Ludhiana, where ARK Imports was supposed to have stored 12,000 tons of raw wool, there was nothing. One borrower had vacated its premises months back, while another refused to admit they owed anything at all.

NSEL's investors involved clients from nearly every major broker in India. Even the Sahara Group, which was under RBI and SEBI scrutiny, was found to have invested more than Rs 200 crore. Some NSEL board members were also close to political bigwigs. CEO Anjani Sinha had earlier in his career overseen defaults in two exchanges in Magadh and Ahmedabad.

Belling this cat will not be an easy task and eight years later, investors are still whistling for their money.

Where are the regulators?

The FMC was supposed to control regulation of all forward contracts. Although NSEL had received an exemption, it was only for T+2 contracts and definitely not the T+35 contracts. The new FMC chief, Ramesh Abhishek, started investigating this in 2012. But what about before him?

The Department of Consumer Affairs was the de facto regulator when no one else was. It had been made aware of the situation over a year before the notification and it should have taken action. But it didn't.

Even after the scam was unearthed, and the scale of the borrowing discovered, regulators remain tight-lipped about action. SEBI has barred some of the twenty-four 'borrowers' from trading on the stock exchange, and FMC has ring-fenced MCX (a commodities futures exchange, which shares the same promoter, FTIL, with NSEL) from helping the beleaguered NSEL with its cash. However, any other actions have yet to come through.

Where is the RBI in this picture? Banks have lent to operations against stocks in warehouses. In fact, some photos of NSEL warehouses explicitly state goods are pledged to certain banks. Are these goods actually there? Has the RBI asked banks to initiate a probe? Not yet as of 2021.

If FTIL was the promoter of NSEL, and NSEL had seen a huge default, the next obvious step was to declare that FTIL was not 'fit and proper' to run any other exchange, including MCX. This duly happened, and MCX was then sold by FTIL.

Were brokers to blame?

Brokers must have known something was rotten. After all, it isn't normal to coordinate a paired buy and sell. Also, brokers are expected to be fiduciary agents of their customers – should they have exercised more caution before recommending such an investment?

Many brokers, however, fell prey to these machinations themselves and succumbed to greed. They promised investors a return of, say, 12 per cent, and then took that money to NSEL and made the 3 per cent extra NSEL promised.

When NSEL defaulted, brokers blamed the exchange. But just like the exchange, they promised money, which they have to pay. SEBI must act and ensure these brokers pay.

Where is the money?

The short answer: We don't know.

The Enforcement Directorate and a Mumbai Police Special Investigations Team (SIT) are trying to find the money. It's gone abroad through hawala, says the SIT. Others claim it was used to fund real estate, where there is no swift liquidity. Yet others claim the money was used to prop up FTIL and MCX shares in the stock market. So when those stocks fell, the amount of money that could be recovered reduced. It is also believed the money was siphoned for political interests, or for personal gains of the personalities involved. Take your pick of the theories!

Jignesh Shah, the ambitious promoter of FTIL, started out as an engineer on the BOLT system for the Bombay Stock Exchange in 1989. After learning the ropes, he set up FTIL in 1995 and established a presence in brokerage back-office and terminal software across India. Then he set up MCX and a slew of other exchanges in India, and abroad.

Shah won a battle against SEBI in 2012 about a circumvention of regulation in their new MCX-SX stock exchange. He had aggressively taken away market share from other exchanges and he was among the first to list a financial exchange. He has sued people who wrote against him, and cultivated media contacts with a big advertising budget. NSEL's exemption from the Department of Consumer Affairs was attributed to Shah's influence.

It would be a surprise if someone with Shah's business sense let all this happen without having a clue where the money has gone.

What happens to MCX and FTIL?

FTIL has now been renamed as 63Moons Technologies. Perhaps that's about how far the money has gone. That share fell sharply, dropping over 70 per cent from its 31 July 2013 price of Rs 540. It derived a large portion of its profits from NSEL – the trades resulted in outsized earnings through exchange fees. But the sudden lack of profit is not its only problem. FTIL was forced to sell its holding of MCX, India's largest commodities forward market exchange.

MCX is a well-regulated exchange. The volumes in it haven't come down quite as much as one would suppose. Its share price fell 60 per cent after NSEL's shutdown announcement on 31 July. Nearly eight years later, in 2021, the share price of MCX remains roughly where it was before the NSEL drama.

The future?

The NSEL crisis showed the investment community one thing: India does not have adequate regulation or enforcement. If there is a crisis, the 'agreement' will not be sacrosanct even if it is legally watertight; it will be secondary to the interests of parties who have political and business connections.

This default triggered other issues, and in a country already branded as 'crony-capitalist', the lack of will to enforce laws and put people in jail for fraud has hampered future investment. Decisive action is required, but the window for action is fast shrinking after eight years of doing nothing.

The problem really is a loss of trust. The entire financial system is based on trust – for example, if everyone tried to withdraw his or her bank deposits at once, we'd have to shut the banking system down. Every attempt to abuse or undermine this trust must be dealt with strongly.

NSEL's 'getting away with it' leaves us all with a deficit of trust and that's much worse than a fiscal deficit or current account deficit.

The basic point here was a proposition that sounded too good to be true. You can't be getting a 'risk-free' 15 per cent a year, when other low-risk avenues give you about 8 per cent max. The risk is bound to be there, hidden, somewhere.

The lunatics: When insanity meets investments

Everyone loves a good investment, but it's even more exciting if it doubles overnight. And that game has existed forever. You'll know this if a cousin, or an old friend, will drop in and tell you how you can double your money and there's no way you can lose. Some of this will actually work, which is why it tempts you. After all, what you need is one good break, and then you can keep the money in fixed deposits because you'll have enough. But in a bull market, what spreads fast is a load of bull.

Here's a list of things we've heard about.

The plantation schemes (teak, etc.)

'Do you want to profit from wood?' asks your friend. You're curious, and it doesn't matter what comes after the word 'profit'.

'Of course, what's the deal?' you ask, hoping it isn't illegal.

'We buy a teak farm,' says the friend. 'Let's plant teak trees and sell them when they mature. It costs Rs 1250 and you'll get fifty kgs of teak and it sells for thousand rupees a kg. That's 5x in profit in twenty years.'

You're mortified. Who in their right minds wants to grow things in a farm, for twenty years? 'I'm not giving up my day job, dude.'

'Precisely,' says your friend. 'Instead of doing this, let's pay a company that owns land, to plant teak for us. They'll grow the teak into a tree, and we'll get the money.'

You go with it, but eventually realize that the company which took the money had no trees, or not enough land, or no intent to actually make good on the promise. Hey, in fifty years, you might be dead anyhow. They get caught, eventually, because someone figures it out, or the cheques start to bounce.

There's many versions of this scam, from teak farms to emus and ostriches.

The scam is eternal – from the 1990s to as recently as 2016, large numbers of people have fallen for such schemes.

MLM schemes

In Mumbai in 2008, I met a person living in our apartment block who wanted to speak with us. He brought his wife along, and gave my wife and me a long spiel about how I could be 'free' if I could run my own business.

The problem, I kept saying, was that I was running my own business, and I had been for the decade before that, and no, it doesn't give you freedom.

But he was insistent. There was an hour of such talk of freedom. After that, we badgered them to please get to the point because our toddler had zero patience for the concept of our freedom. The point was simple: I had to sign on to some multi-level marketing scheme, and buy soaps or shampoos, but also recruit other people like they were doing. The 'downline' revenue – a percentage of what everyone in the network recruited by you and then onward – would be so substantial you could retire many times over!

As you've probably realized by now, he was pushing me to join Amway, which is a worldwide 'network marketing' company, a concept otherwise known as multi-level marketing (MLM). After a very long and frustratingly meandering discussion,

Amway turned out to be this company selling consumer goods like shampoos, detergents and dietary supplements.

You were supposed to join a 'programme' where you paid a fee, and used these products or sold them to your friends. You got a commission on every sale, and if you enrolled any of your friends into the programme, you got a piece of their pie as well. The products were overpriced, but supposedly fabulous. I was then propositioned to join, and in the manner of all politely bankrupt individuals, I smiled and refused.

That was fortunate. Although I hear a number of individuals have made substantial amounts of money being Amway superheroes, MLM wouldn't work for a person like me. And the reason is emotional – I cherish friendships and relationships to the point that I neither want to sell, or be sold anything, especially if it's overpriced shampoo.

MLM, on the face of it, is noble – you get a piece of what you would spend anyway, and you get to build an organization ('downline') which keeps feeding you money back as it grows. But the specifics in the real world muddy the waters.

First, the products tend to be quite expensive – this is the case with at least three MLM organizations I've seen. The pitch here is that the products are superior, and in any case you make some of the money back. But even with the 20 per cent kickback, paying Rs 125 for toothpaste isn't very financially sound when regular FMCG competitors are at Rs 50, and I'm not sure how 'advanced' you can get with toothpaste.

Second, the MLM recruits are pushed to get new people into the organization, because just 'selling products' doesn't do much. An Amway 'Sales and Marketing Plan' builds scale primarily from getting more people into your 'downline' organization. Additionally, you get a fancier designation as you get more people in. Selling a product is a far easier proposition than trying to get someone else to enrol, and the incentive to enrol new folks ensures most distributors don't care about selling the product. Indeed, in their eagerness, the good people who designed the Amway brochures decided that the average family of four would need protein powder, multi-vitamins and dietary supplements collectively worth Rs 3500 a month, which is unfathomable to other residents of India.

Third, people in the organization are encouraged to sell at every opportunity they get; and because they try to enrol people they know well – remember, you can't put up a shop and sell to total strangers under the MLM model – they end up with relationship pain; from disgust, to suspicion of their motives, every single time. This causes almost universal hatred of anything MLM, probably from the feeling of being scammed as the MLMers start their spiel with offering freedom and end with an entry fee to sell soap.

Lastly, instead of product sales, a new way to make money seems to have become popular: Selling 'tools'. Once you're in, you'll find someone in the hierarchy will have built motivational tapes, or will be charging for his/her seminars. Paying for this adds substantially to your cost, and might make a great return for someone up the line. (How do you know what was paid for that fancy car?) A DateLine video revealed how prevalent this was.

Eric Scheibeler wrote the book *Merchants of Deception*, describing his experiences as an 'Emerald' distributor in the business. It reveals dark, dirty details of how the product sales concept was twisted into a mentally manipulative system, making people work far more than they expected to (weekends included), earn a lot less money than they imagined, buy tapes and attend seminars and never question the 'system'. If that sounds like a cult, it's what many MLM schemes have been described as.

Many confuse MLM with a Ponzi scheme, which is inaccurate. Charles Ponzi (and more recently, Bernie Madoff) would borrow from investors promising high interest rates, and use subsequent investors' money to pay off the earlier investors. At some point the scheme blew up as the rate of flow of new investors slowed.

In a way this is how a pyramid scheme operates – where you only get paid if you enlist more people, which can get out of hand pretty fast; where you're pitched that you can make ridiculous amounts of money by enrolling just six more people, understand that if this concept started with you and went to thirteen levels deep, you're talking about enrolling more than twice the world population! But all MLMs aren't pyramid schemes; companies like Amway make a lot more money from product sales, versus entry fees.

MLM recruits tend to oversupply themselves with the products, in order to keep their grades. I've heard horror stories of people who spent lakhs of rupees buying products so they could keep their 'Ruby' status; and now there is way too much toothpaste or detergent to even consider healthy competition.

But this attitude is not limited to the MLM industry. I have had mutual fund agents ask me to buy a product just to make a sales number, where they would refund any losses on immediate redemption – they needed the sales to qualify for a company-paid trip to Dubai – the idea being that the trip was worth a little money, even if it was just an incentive.

I wouldn't recommend the business, unless it's to consume their products. (For the record, I've been a user of Amway and Tupperware products.) You're at the mercy of a large organization that pays you based on business from your downlines, and your sense of 'freedom' may be immediately shot to pieces if you do something they don't like, such as not buying their products or violating their changing guidelines – this dependence is not exactly compatible with retirement.

You can't get more productive, like sell to the masses over the web or at a shop, a strange restriction. People higher up in the hierarchy seem to work even harder than you, inconsistent with the pitch you were given. And finally, the negativity you are likely to generate in your social circle is simply not worth it.

Single-level marketing programmes – like Affiliate marketing at e-commerce sites – has the MLM benefits and there is no impetus to hire more people into the network.

If you're not a part of an MLM organization and don't want to be, remember that the more time someone takes to come to 'how much does it cost?' the more likely it's going to be an MLM concept. And just like ULIPs, it's easy to argue that the companies aren't bad, the salespeople mis-sell – but that doesn't fly with me, as these companies have ignored such complaints in the past. The unfortunate consequence as they attempt to reform is that they are saddled with the past image of deception and the abuse of persuasion.

The cryptocurrency scams

We've suddenly seen the advent of bitcoin. This is a cryptocurrency. The reason it's called crypto is that no one understands it because it's so cryptic.

I'm kidding, of course. But only slightly. Because the price of bitcoin keeps going up! And bitcoin is passe. Now there's other coins which are going up even faster.

The concept of crypto is that you have a digital form of currency that is unique to each holder, and placed on a common 'blockchain' – a ledger in which you have all transactions of all bitcoin all over the world, since the beginning of bitcoin. This is secured by cryptographic algorithmic security that is difficult to crack. Anyone can download a blockchain, so it's a distributed framework of blockchains that holds the transaction records of bitcoin.

The total amount of bitcoin in the world is limited, so it's imperative that over time its price will go up against the dollar or rupee. It has – rising to US$60,000 per bitcoin in March 2021 from a mere US$7000 in January 2020. This is the stuff of legends, so obviously people want to be a part of it.

Due to bitcoin's limited supply, there's other 'shitcoin' (their real name!) which emerges from the shadows. One crypto algorithm is called bitcoin. Another respected one is Ethereum. But to attract the loonies, people created currencies, just as a joke, like Dogecoin. That coin went up 300 per cent in 2021 alone (January to June).

Enough people are attracted to such returns in the hopes of pulling off one big trade that will change their lives. Ten Doge falls 50 per cent in four weeks and if you were the sucker that bought near the top, you're just going to have to call it the cost of an education.

Forex and options

The concept of leverage sounds attractive. Put up Rs 100 and if something goes up 1 per cent, your money becomes Rs 200. Effectively, you have 100x leverage. The problem is that if it goes DOWN 1 per cent, your Rs 100 goes to zero.

You'll hear about a lot of leveraged products. Forex – or foreign exchange futures trading – for one, is an extremely popular concept. There are advertisements for exchanges abroad that allow forex trading, in currencies like the US dollar versus the Japanese yen (currencies are always quoted one against the other).

You get a lot of leverage on these products. A Rs 1000 bet can expose you to currency worth Rs 1,00,000 – 100x times. This means that if the currency bet goes in your direction, you will gain very large sums relative to your 'margin' money. But since it's a double-edged sword, you also lose heavily when the market goes against you.

Options trading is similar, but usually not as richly leveraged. When you buy an option, you get the right to buy something at a particular price (called a strike price) at some day in the future (called the maturity date, this is often the expiry date as well) or within a certain time frame before the contract expires.

Options are available on lots of different 'underlying' assets, ranging from individual stocks to forex to stock indices. Some are 'European' – only to be exercised on the expiry date; others are 'American' and can be exercised any time before expiry.

A call option allows you to buy an asset, while a put option gives you the right but not the obligation to sell at a given strike price. So if you think the asset is going to rise in price, you can buy a call, and vice versa you can buy a put if you think the asset is going to drop.

You pay a certain amount, called a premium, for buying such an option – it's the privilege of having the right, but not the obligation, to buy something at that price on, or before maturity date. The idea is: If the market doesn't go up to the strike price, you don't buy, since you're not obliged to, and you only lose the premium.

An option seller, however, is on the other side, so he has an obligation to sell that same thing at the strike price on the obligation date. But he receives the premium upfront, as compensation for the effort.

The common thought is that buying options is a losing game, and most option buyers are statistically likely to lose their premium (i.e., the underlying asset doesn't move enough). If that is so, then there's money in selling options. But option selling is like this: For a few months, you'll make money because the underlying asset doesn't move enough.

But suddenly in one month the underlying's price will move fast, and in that month you'll lose so much that you give back all your profits. In general, a reckless blind mechanism of selling options will work in a range-bound market, but when there's a big price-trend against you, there will be a massive loss.

In 2011, a friend was enamoured by the lure of profits in option selling, and provided Rs 1.5 crore as capital to a brokerage company which said it excelled in it. For the first year, he received 2 per cent a month – a fairly large amount even in 2011 – and my friend was excited. I was asked to analyse the trades, and when I did, I only said this: I hope they don't lose their mind because this is a game of discipline. When the range is very narrow, they could get overaggressive and take on more risk than they should.

That's what happened. One year later, the friend called me saying that the Rs 1.5 crore was now a mere Rs 80 lakh – falling by nearly half, even after including the monthly 2 per cent payoffs he had received. I looked at the trades again, and found that over time, the 2 per cent per month reduced to 1 per cent per month, and to get it back up to 2 per cent, the broker took on more leverage. Just after the broker did that, the market exploded up and then fell. That hurt the option strategy so much that the losses ate up a whole year's worth of profit!

Options and forex trades are about discipline. This is a lesson not learnt easily, except in the school of hard knocks.

Acknowledgements

This book would not have been possible without the help, support and patience of many people, and I wish to acknowledge their contributions although I know I'll never do enough justice with mere words. But words are all we have, as Samuel Beckett said, famously acknowledged in tune by the band Boyzone.

I thank the awesome team at Capitalmind, where I work, for providing their valuable feedback and support. My thanks to Shray, Vashistha, Anoop, Akanksha, Sandeep, Krishna, Priyanka and Varun for their inputs and thoughts on what is a dry topic.

I must thank Devangshu Datta, a friend and mentor, for his efforts in helping shape the book and for agreeing to edit the early draft of the book, and to make the language more readable. DD is a legend, and I would do him a disfavour by stopping praise for him at any point, but suffice it to say I'm grateful for all the time he put into making this book meaningful.

My thanks to the brilliant folks at Juggernaut for putting the book together. Chiki, thanks for being focused on ensuring this book actually happens and for driving me to keep at it.

My dad would have loved this book, and would have been proud to see his engineer son write about markets. Dad, I miss you very much. Amma, I'm deeply grateful for everything you've done for me.

I couldn't have done this without the support of Varun and Zubin, my two not-so-little-any more boys, who don't want anything to do with finance and I'm glad for that. My greatest source of support, joy and happiness is my wife, Sunila, who is Wonder Woman and doesn't know it, and if I had to really tell you what I'm thankful for, that would be another – and more interesting – book. But that's the book we'll write together, S.

A Note on the Author

Deepak Shenoy is CEO at Capitalmind, a SEBI registered portfolio manager that manages over Rs 500 crore in the Indian markets. His views on investing have appeared in *Business Standard*, Moneycontrol and other media. He is a regular guest on CNBC TV18 and ET Now and has spoken at various investment conferences. For more, you can visit https://capitalmind.in.

A startup founder since 1998, Deepak is happy to embrace risk for greater reward. He loves to write, decode complexity and learn new things, not always finance. He lives in Bengaluru with his family.

juggernaut

THE APP FOR INDIAN READERS

Fresh, original books tailored for mobile and for India. Starting at ₹10.

juggernaut.in

1

CRAFTED FOR MOBILE READING

Thought you would never read a book on mobile? Let us prove you wrong.

juggernaut.in

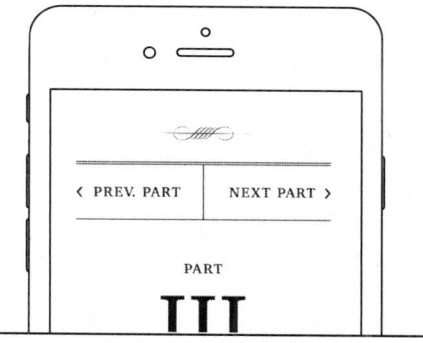

Beautiful Typography

The quality of print transferred to your mobile. Forget ugly PDFs.

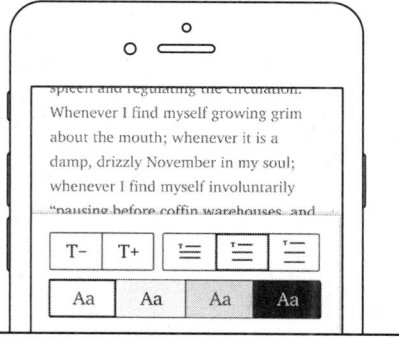

Customizable Reading

Read in the font size, spacing and background of your liking.

juggernaut.in

AN EXTENSIVE LIBRARY

Including fresh, new, original Juggernaut books from the likes of Sunny Leone, Praveen Swami, Husain Haqqani, Umera Ahmed, Rujuta Diwekar and lots more. Plus, books from partner publishers and loads of free classics. Whichever genre you like, there's a book waiting for you.

juggernaut.in

juggernaut.in

DON'T JUST READ; INTERACT

We're changing the reading experience from passive to active.

juggernaut.in

Ask authors questions

Get all your answers from the horse's mouth. Juggernaut authors actually reply to every question they can.

Rate and review

Let everyone know of your favourite reads or critique the finer points of a book – you will be heard in a community of like-minded readers.

Gift books to friends

For a book-lover, there's no nicer gift than a book personally picked. You can even do it anonymously if you like.

Enjoy new book formats

Discover serials released in parts over time, picture books including comics, and story-bundles at discounted rates. And coming soon, audiobooks.

juggernaut.in

Click the QR Code with a QR scanner app or type the link into the Internet browser on your phone to download the Juggernaut app.

For our complete catalogue, visit www.juggernaut.in
To submit your book, send a synopsis and two sample chapters to books@juggernaut.in
For all other queries, write to contact@juggernaut.in